A GELATO A DAY

MIROLAND IMPRINT 36

Guernica Editions Inc. acknowledges the support of the Canada Council for the Arts and the Ontario Arts Council. The Ontario Arts Council is an agency of the Government of Ontario.

We acknowledge the financial support of the Government of Canada.

A GELATO A DAY

Edited by

CLAUDIA LAROYE

MiroLand
publishers
MIROLAND (GUERNICA)
TORONTO—CHICAGO—BUFFALO—LANCASTER (U.K.)
2022

Guernica Founder: Antonio D'Alfonso

Connie McParland, series editor
Michael Mirolla, editor
Cover and interior design: Errol F. Richardson
Guernica Editions Inc.
287 Templemead Drive, Hamilton, ON L8W 2W4
2250 Military Road, Tonawanda, N.Y. 14150-6000 U.S.A.
www.guernicaeditions.com

Distributors:
Independent Publishers Group (IPG)
600 North Pulaski Road, Chicago IL 60624
University of Toronto Press Distribution (UTP)
5201 Dufferin Street, Toronto (ON), Canada M3H 5T8
Gazelle Book Services
White Cross Mills, High Town, Lancaster LA1 4XS U.K.

First edition.

Legal Deposit—Third Quarter
Library of Congress Catalog Card Number: 2021949998
Library and Archives Canada Cataloguing in Publication
Title: A gelato a day / edited by Claudia Laroye.
Names: Laroye, Claudia, editor.
Identifiers: Canadiana (print) 2021037067X | Canadiana (ebook) 20210370688 |
ISBN 9781771836180 (softcover) | ISBN 9781771836944 (EPUB)
Subjects: CSH: Travelers' writings, Canadian (English). | LCSH: Travelers' writings,
American.
Classification: LCC G465 .G45 2022 | DDC 910.4—dc23

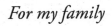
For my family

CONTENTS

FOREWORD

If you're a parent, did you ever get that dreadful feeling of thinking the free-spirited travelling life of your youth would suddenly be reduced to having to choose between Disney Theme Parks, all-inclusive resorts with kids' clubs, and family road trips to National Parks? That your days of roaming freely to wherever you wanted to go or using your passport were put on standby until the kids graduated high school?

Don't get me wrong. There's absolutely nothing wrong with these aforementioned vacation options as they are each wonderful to do with your kids. It's just the feeling that venturing too far and wide with children isn't really the right thing to do—or even feasible.

The reality is that having children doesn't mean your choices when travelling become more limited. Quite the opposite in fact. You'll be relieved to know that starting a family will ultimately broaden your horizons of where, how, and even why to travel.

From my own experiences and subsequent writings on the subject, I've learned that parents who are willing to take on the challenges of travelling with children are rewarded in ways they never would have expected.

You can't put a price tag on seeing the joy in your child's eyes the first time they see "the real" Mickey Mouse in Orlando; it's just as thrilling to see "the real" Cinderella's Castle in Bavaria years later. Or the exhilaration that comes from mom, dad, and the kids putting on their masks and snorkels to swim together with tropical fish in the Caribbean.

I remember watching in amazement as my eight-year old son lit some incense and gently offered it and a prayer to a statue of Buddha inside a Chinese temple. And I couldn't help but reignite that long lost magic of the holiday spirit when we strolled through the Christmas Markets of Germany, warming up with some hot chocolate and Glühwein.

Moments like these are only a few examples of how vacationing as a family can be just as transformational as it is recreational, for the kids and for yourselves. Above all else, these travel experiences bring a family closer together, something that is often taken for granted or assumed, and remains so important to every member of the family.

There are so many benefits of travelling as a family. Exposing the kids to new cultures and perspectives is certainly one of them. Allowing children to go beyond the confines and familiarity of their hometowns will only heighten their sense of curiosity and wonder, and foster self-esteem and independence.

Vacations can strengthen a child's connection to the natural world, a relationship that is increasingly important for fostering environmental stewardship. There is always the potential to form life-long lasting friendships with the people you meet along the way. And of course, family travel will enrich a child's education and teach them new life skills. Snowboarding, horseback riding, and learning to sail are examples of things we've tried for the first time while on holiday.

Perhaps my biggest surprise was seeing how our travels with the kids promoted a sense of self-discovery. How we didn't just explore the world around us, but ourselves as well. Had it not been for travelling so much with my children, I probably never would have started writing about our adventures—never mind creating the Family Travel Association in 2014. Following many years of travelling together, my son's passion for aeronautics blossomed and now his first job after graduating college is with SpaceX. But ultimately, the key is togetherness and memory-making, no matter where or how families travel.

There's a reason the writers and their essays selected for this anthology made the cut. They are gifted storytellers who can craft a narrative that reinforces the unique power and value of travelling as a family while making the reader want to follow in their footsteps. The literary journey these stories navigate ranges from comical pieces about travelling with toddlers, thought-provoking family trips to faraway lands, to serious accounts of parent-adult child bonding and the revelations of family histories. These tales will take you on an adventure from Bhutan to the northern wilds of Canada and Soviet Russia, Hawaii to Costa Rica, Kenya and beyond, and the timelines are similarly wide-ranging.

By presenting an anthology of some of her favourite work on the subject, Claudia masterfully showcases 'the good, bad and the ugly' of the family travel experience. How it can be crazy, hilarious, wonderful, chaotic, poignant and wonderfully meaningful, and above all worthwhile in the undertaking.

At its best, travelling with family can change our perception of ourselves, our loved ones, and the world around us. These travel stories are as significant as tales of individual self-discovery, illuminating the beautiful complexity of human interaction and connection that takes place within a family, no matter how big, small, structured or dysfunctional it may be.

Rainer Jenss
Founder, Family Travel Association

INTRODUCTION

We travel in part, to shake our complacencies.
—Pico Iyer

Nothing shakes complacencies more than travelling with one's children. No matter how in control you may have been in your previous child-free life, or how hard and fast you white-knuckle grip onto any semblance of control once baby arrives and morphs into toddler, child and beyond, circumstances out of that control will work, often actively, against you.

Where is the joy in that? Well, truthfully, there are times when the joy is deeply buried, underneath piles of laundry, tears and fatigue. Life is always a roller coaster of highs and lows, peaks and valleys of emotion. When children become part of our lives, those feelings can intensify to overwhelming levels: protection brings out our core human instincts.

Travelling with family isn't really about shaking complacencies, though that will happen. At its best, family travel can be about education, memory-making and spending time together in places near and far from home. Whether in comfort or conflict, travel with family members teaches us something about ourselves and those we love, whom fate, choice or genetics have flung together. As writer Bruce Kirkby argues in his essay, it takes children to shake the complacencies from our travel.

My first trip with my family occurred at the tender age of one. My parents and I were flying to Europe to visit my maternal grandparents. In an effort to ensure a smooth flight, my mother had given me Gravol, an anti-nausea medication that, in addition to limiting air sickness, would knock me out for the six-hour journey.

It had the opposite effect. I was awake and alert, gleefully running down the aisles of the plane with my mother chasing me. My father sought refuge in the back, pretending not to know us. He managed to sleep and arrived rested while my mother greeted her family in a state of exhaustion.

While I don't remember any of this, I believe it happened and love the story. Our trip was about me, but it wasn't about me remembering every moment. After all, I was just one year old. The trip was about my family, about introducing me to family members who most assuredly remembered the moments we spent together. And that was the point. The act of travel was a bonding exercise; an initiation into a larger entity of belonging.

At its core, travelling with family is a case of planning for the best, and preparing for the worst. No matter how far away the destination or how long the journey, the keys to family travel success lie in planning and preparation. Liberally sprinkled with large doses of patience, resilience and a sense of humour when and if it all goes to hell.

The title for this book came from a phrase that I conceived when my children were very young, created during a five-week European adventure in the early 2000s. The strategy behind *a gelato a day keeps the tantrums away* was simple. Offer a daily incentive of a favoured treat on every day of a trip, to promote anticipation, happiness and motivation to get through the day. After all, who doesn't like ice cream?

The enticement worked like a charm, keeping us from meltdowns (from both young and old) while wandering narrow mediaeval streets in Belgium and during long mountain hikes in the Swiss Alps. It was so successful that, towards the end of our trip, our youngest was sick of gelato and instead begged for a daily cake substitute.

Travelling with kids and family members isn't really about sweet bribes for good behaviour, though believe me, they can work wonders. For all of its possible complexities, family travel is about spending time together in ways that can amaze, delight, sadden and sometimes even shock individual members. It can illuminate histories, teach stewardship of cultures, wildlife and the environment, and create life-long memories that generate laughter or tears decades after the experience has taken place.

This collection of stories highlights the good, the bad and the not-really-that ugly of family travel. The travelling tales go beyond holidays-gone-wrong to dive thoughtfully into the deeper parental and family connections that can occur when we take ourselves (or are taken out of) our daily routines and comfort zones. More often than not, entering unfamiliar places, spaces and situations encourages us to open up to one another or react in ways that may surprise, delight or frustrate those we hold most dear. As writer Alec Scott puts it so well in his piece, we take ourselves out of our respective routines, look up and see each other, hopefully liking what we see.

In this anthology, many stories speak to the value and worth of travelling with children to far-flung places, even when 'they won't remember it.' As humans are strongly shaped by connections and learning that occurs before the age of five, our authors agree with developmental experts that the intrinsic value of travelling with young children speaks for itself.

Several tales involve adult children travelling with parents who reveal sides of themselves that surprise and astonish, ultimately serving to strengthen familial bonds and recognition of parents as individuals rather than servants to their children's existence.

The stories roam the world from Asia to the Amazon, Nantucket to Kenya and all the places in-between. They also travel through the space-time continuum, harkening back to the Soviet Union in the 1980s, wartime Italy, post-colonial Morocco, and the American Midwest circa 1954. The familiar and exotic locations serve as backdrops for stories of how travel illuminates the people we think we know—ourselves, our kids and our parents.

Other tales revolve around the joy, wonder, stress and chaos that come when one travels with children, particularly of the younger set. Think of mild 'Toddlers Gone Wild' scenes, or lessons learned from teenagers released from the confines of peer groups and WiFi. These stories aren't meant to scare off parents from attempting travel with their young ones. Rather, they're an honest portrayal of what family travel looks like; that even at its most challenging, it's absolutely still worth the effort.

Reading and editing these stories during a pandemic was a strange and otherworldly experience. While I was grateful for the time at home to do the necessary work of producing a book of travel stories, reading these travel tales made me long, keenly and desperately, for the act of travel itself; the freedom to pick a destination, to board a plane and fly away, to visit and be with family and friends. If nothing else, I will never take the ability to travel—with or without my family—for granted ever again.

Consider this anthology a road map to the wonderful experiences that travelling with family can provide when we give ourselves over to the magic of spending time with the people we love, away from the confines of daily life. Through travel, we discover new things about ourselves, our world and each other, creating precious memories that will live on long after the suitcases are unpacked and the laundry folded away.

Claudia Laroye
Vancouver, Canada

THE UNEXPECTED JOYS AND WONDERS OF TRAVEL WITH KIDS

Bruce Kirkby

Many have asked, in the years since I took my young family to live a Himalayan Buddhist monastery, if I regretted dragging children so young on such a long and arduous journey? Do they remember anything of those days? Did it change them in any measurable or quantifiable way? Was it worth the effort?

There is nearly always a tone of scepticism accompanying such queries, and what I suspect they are really trying to ask is: just how badly did it suck?

Such an outlook never fails to surprise and sadden me.

Travel with young children is broadly seen as the modern equivalent of a hair shirt; a penance preferably avoided, or at best, endured.

Kids, it is held, with their whining and restlessness and tantrums, dilute the inherent joys of wandering so profoundly that the resulting experience is, at best, a lukewarm rendition of the real thing, incomparable to the eye-opening, heart-stretching miracle that was youthful-travel-before-parenthood.

Meaningful family journeys (never mind enjoyable) are widely regarded as a myth; the unattainable dream of selfish parents, and a bloody nuisance for everyone else.

Yet despite dire warnings and incessant dissuasion, many young parents still choose to set off with kids in tow. Those initial journeys are, generally, acts of defiance. The road is in their blood. Unwilling or unable to surrender this faith, they book tickets, clinging to that worn mantra: "Parenthood won't change me."

They are, of course, wrong.

But their trust in travel—in the inherent good that comes from exploring unfamiliar worlds, both within and abroad—does not misguide them, for even as the road brings whispers of past hopes and dreams to the parents, it also gently shapes and nourishes their inquisitive child. Perhaps most significantly, the time away from distractions and 'real life,' with all its uncertainties and challenges and enchantments, acts like fertilizer on a young family's nascent bonds.

The first thing a travelling parent will notice is the unsettling abundance of time; minutes and hours and days that cannot be filled with the usual knickknacks of home.

Consider this: Woken by roosters, you wander the unfamiliar avenues of a foreign city for hours, young child perched happily atop your shoulders. Together you have eaten breakfast, walked some more, stopped for coffee, and later shared an ice cream. You have played I-Spy to the point of exhaustion. Then you glance at your watch, and discover it is only 8 in the morning.

The horror! What in god's good name will you do for the rest of the day?

Your brain and body scream for sleep, but the more pressing your need to lie down, even for a just a moment, the less likely your children are to slow their pace.

Yet as the hours crawl by, it dawns that you have been holding those little hands longer, and more often, than you ordinarily would at home. Above the din of bus stations and markets, you begin to take note of your child's hushed commentary, something often lost amid the hue and cry of the daily home struggle. You linger together, shoulder to shoulder, marvelling over the tang of wild raspberries plucked from a roadside bush, or the deep toll of a cathedral's bell.

'We travel in part,' Pico Iyer famously said, 'to shake our complacencies.'

I would argue it takes children to shake the complacencies from our travel. Routines and habits developed over a lifetime of backpacking journeys are tossed the instant we touch down, for children race down every road and path but the ones we'd instinctively follow. More interested in chickens and graffiti than Internet cafés and landmarks, they can happily pass an entire afternoon watching a construction site or playing hopscotch. And the gems such restlessness unearths—a Hong Kong sushi bar where the waiters are dressed as Asian cartoon characters, a crumbling Soviet amusement park crowded with Kazakh families—are rarely found in any guidebook.

As we chase in our children's wake, we approach strangers we'd normally avoid, and knock on doors that would otherwise remain closed, because children's simplest needs—food, sleep, bathroom breaks—arrive with undebatable urgency. And a parent's sheepish grins and bungled attempts at sign language are now met with open arms and sympathetic grins, revealing the greatest gift children bestow on travel: common ground. Being a parent isn't easy. And everyone—from Bhutanese villagers to Milanese businessmen—knows it.

In the planet's far-flung corners, we rarely share language, religion or even cultural outlook with those we wander amongst. Our backpacks and suitcases carry riches the locals may never know; our lives awash with opportunities they'll never realize. We live, literally, a world apart. Yet with the cry of a baby, or the blink of a child, such barriers tumble away.

Suddenly, taxi drivers begin inviting you home for dinner. Construction workers leap from scaffolding to tickle a little one. Teenage boys stop horsing about and politely ask to hold your baby, whom you nervously pass, and whom they take as gently and lovingly as a grandmother. We find ourselves sitting at kitchen tables, breaking bread, playing impromptu soccer, chasing chickens, singing songs, inspecting heirlooms and raising glasses, all with the constant awareness: I would never experience such precious moments were it not for my children.

Children—both ours and theirs—speak of common hopes and common struggles, and there just may be no more unifying a human bond.

Rather than insulating us from opportunity on the road—as many accuse —our kids create it instead, at a dizzying rate.

One lament travelling parents hear again and again is this: "What a pity they won't remember any of it."

The implication being that somehow the cost of getting kids halfway around the world (and perhaps the effort) has been wasted without lifelong memories to show for it.

Such sentiment is understandable, for it's hard to imagine that the effects of hitchhiking across Australia, or boarding a river boat in the Congo, could be more profound and enduring for a three-year-old (who won't remember the trip in later life) than the same journey, undertaken by the same girl, at the age of 21 (when she will carry fond memories for the rest of her years).

Yet every shred of evidence suggests the early years are at very least equally influential—if not more.

Unconvinced?

Then take an infant to Buenos Aires, or Kathmandu, or Siem Reap, or any foreign land where children are woven through the strands of daily life, where strangers approach ceaselessly—poking, tickling and whispering to the baby, without so much as a sideways glance at you. Suddenly, the African proverb "It takes a village to raise a child" becomes more than a line on a card. (For Western parents of course, this challenges our ingrained instinct to monitor and filter every interaction our babies have). Within days, the infant has learned to seek the attention of strangers, basking in their affection.

To watch the process in reverse is heartbreaking. Board a plane bound for Canada with an infant, and the collective aversion of eyes is obvious. Ditto for walking into a restaurant back at home. The child, of course, will continue to wave and coo at strangers, in cafés and supermarkets, although far fewer will return the attention. Eventually, the baby gives up.

Travelling parents are also warned incessantly of the conditions their children will face. Pollution! Noise! Filth! Poverty, theft, and spicy food.

But our kids are so much more resilient than we ever give them credit for. All they need is the foundation of their parent's love. Keep them fed, dressed and rested, and they can rise above almost any hurdle.

When things fall apart, as they often do on the road, when we get royally ripped off, or the bus breaks down and the air conditioning fails, pause and take note of who is upset. Most likely it's the parents, for it is we who feel the need to control every detail of our days. And it is our kids, with their Buddha-like acceptance, who remind us that such trivialities rarely matter.

Through these ups and downs, these trials and frustrations, we are laid bare to our children's scrutiny. And far more important than what we do in these moments of challenge, is how we do it. I am aware that the presence of my young boys brings out a better traveller in me than I previously knew existed.

Admittedly, when things go wrong with the kids themselves—illness, exhaustion, low blood sugar—the situation can feel precarious. But this is no different than at home, and no reason to stay there.

We travel with our children because we want them to experience first-hand the beauty, sadness and infinite variety of the world. We hope to inoculate them against prejudice, imbue them with curiosity and nurture the practice of lifelong learning. And, along the way, disrupted from circumstance, the family itself grows more tangible.

But such rationalization misses the fundamental humanity of it. To travel with kids is to know them sleeping on your chest, open-mouthed, on a jolting bus. It is to wander dark streets lit by neon lights, hand in hand, both beset with jet lag.

To travel with kids is to be reminded of their infinite trust and be humbled by their essential faith in the goodness of the world.

Travel returns each of us, in a small measure, to a state of childhood. For a fleeting moment, we look out upon the world—crowded with the unrecognizable and incomprehensible—from the same shore as our kids. And, in doing so, the distance between us shrinks, just a bit.

So no, the honest to goodness truth is it didn't suck travelling halfway around the world by surface, with a three-year-old and a seven-year-old in tow, to live for six months in an eight-foot by eight-foot mud brick room, plastered to cliffs above the union of two Himalayan rivers, lost in a swirl of peaks and contested borders where India, Pakistan and China collide. It didn't suck at all.

And yes, I'd do it again.

* * *

Bruce Kirkby is a wilderness writer and adventure photographer recognized for connecting wild places with contemporary issues. With journeys spanning more than eighty countries and thirty years, Kirkby's accomplishments include the first modern crossing of Arabia's Empty Quarter by camel, a descent of Ethiopia's Blue Nile Gorge by raft, a sea kayak traverse of Borneo's northern coast and a coast-to-coast Icelandic trek. A former columnist for The Globe and Mail, *author of three bestselling books, and winner of multiple National Magazine Awards, Kirkby's work has appeared in the* New York Times, Outside *magazine and* Canadian Geographic. *He makes his home in Kimberley, British Columbia.*

A CHILD EXPLORER IN THE AMAZON

Sabine K. Bergmann

Dad's duffel bag was permanently damaged, but it was a small price to pay to meet a superhero, in my opinion.

"Now I see why they warned us!" my mother said, sighing.

As always, Mom was right: The locals who met our group of explorers had indeed warned us. Shortly after we arrived at our new residence in the green tangle of jungle along the Tambopata Amazon tributary, they showed us to our thatched accommodations and pointed out the thick metal safe in our bedroom.

"Leave your valuables—money, jewellery—wherever you like. They will be safe here. But your food, your food you must store in the strongbox."

In the explorer's tradition of arrogance, however, we did not heed their warning. Weary after hours of travel upstream in canoes, we collapsed in the main lodge to recover. It wasn't until after Dad had indulged in a few cocktails (another explorer tradition, I'm told) that he remembered.

"The banana!" he exclaimed.

It was my mother who ventured back across the timber bridge with her flashlight to rescue the bag. She was the one who heard the scratching from the floor, the one who overturned the duffel and leapt, shrieking, into the air at the sight of the palm-sized beetle. By the time Dad and I had returned to our cabin, the encounter was over.

My parents had joined in alliance against the insect. I seemed to be the only one who recognized the superhero strength and persistence this particular arthropod had used to chew through the scissor-proof canvas. As I marvelled at the egg-sized opening,

I imagined what life would be like if I had the strength to break through walls at will.

These, I realized, were the best weeks of my school year.

* * *

My sixth-grade teachers were remarkably flexible when it came to my family's South American adventure. They made a deal with my parents: After missing three full weeks of school, not only would I write a report on Peru, but I would also give an hour-long presentation to the entire middle school. This was an intimidating undertaking: In my eleven years on earth, I had never taught a class.

In preparation, I bought two lined notebooks, a pouch of pencils and three rolls of slide film. During our 23-day excursion, my mother's advice echoed in my brain: "Think of Peru as a living classroom," she had said, "and the tour guides as your substitute teachers."

There was plenty to learn. Our jungle lodge—a collection of lawns and cabins with no electricity or hot water—was a tidy anomaly in one of the largest undeveloped areas in the Amazon basin. The jungle was swarming with life: Hummingbirds and macaws flitted and glided by; walking sticks and tree frogs popped out of their camouflage; monkeys screeched from towering trees. In the evenings, I reviewed my notes under the oil lamps in the main lodge, poring over my drawings of rain forest ecology and the indigenous lore of thorns and weeds and tree spirits.

The only way my classmates would understand this place, I realized, was if I described not only the jungle, but the experience of being in the jungle. They would understand the size of the rivers only if I told them it took forty minutes to cross them in a wooden motorized canoe; they would understand the amount of dirt in the water only if I told them the eddies looked like swirling pools of my mom's milky morning coffees.

"There's too much stuff to talk about!" I wailed from our cabin's porch on the second afternoon. "We haven't even gone to Machu Picchu yet! There's no way I can fit this in one class."

Within seconds, cascades of water began to stream from the sky, slapping the ground so hard that I dropped my notes on the floor. Mom chuckled.

"You'll just have to pick the parts you like the best!" she yelled over the roar of the rain.

* * *

I couldn't quite understand why we needed to wake up at three in the morning. The fact that breakfast was scheduled for 4:30 a.m. didn't make sense either. When I asked, I was told by the collective adult alliance that our group of explorers had an itinerary to stick to.

By mid-morning, we had arrived in the Urubamba Gorge, a forested gully with a narrow, frothing river, just below Machu Picchu.

"Machu Picchu means big peak," our tour guide, Washington, told us. "The city is at 7,000 feet of elevation," he continued, pointing up a steep road of switchbacks, "close to the god of creation."

I turned a page loudly in my notebook, and Washington glanced down at my scribbling pencil. "They called this god *kon titi wiracocha pacha yachachi*," he said, smiling as my pencil stopped short.

Our group spent five hours threading through stone temples and gates as Washington lectured on sun cycles and farming and offerings. But it wasn't until we returned to Machu Picchu in the silence of dawn the following morning that I really felt the place.

Under a pink morning sky, I scrambled behind dad's khaki shorts on the smooth stones of the ruins, stopping alongside him as he marvelled. Soon, I wandered off by myself, walking between ancient walls, imagining ancient peoples. I pictured the sunlight that once streamed through temple windows at solstice, the statues that once stood in the stone niches, the crops that once grew on the terraces.

A couple weeks later, I donned an alpaca hat covered in llama designs and stood before all the sixth-, seventh- and eighth graders to give my presentation.

"This," I said, pointing to a slide of Machu Picchu's ruins, "was my classroom two Thursdays ago."

* * *

Mom had said to pick the parts I liked best. The thing was, I liked all of it.

So, following explorer tradition, I stretched my initial expedition into a life-long pursuit. I continued to study jungles in traditional and untraditional classrooms, ultimately gaining a degree in environmental science. I moved to Bolivia and became fluent in Spanish. I joined the Peace Corps and lived in a thatched cabin in the forest. I carry notebooks everywhere.

As it turns out, being a student of the world can be a real-life career, although there are more pitches and deadlines and copy editors than I realized there would be. Other than that, not too much has changed since I was eleven years old: I still learn incredible things from incredible people, and I still look for superheroes—no matter their size.

* * *

Sabine K. Bergmann *is the co-founder and co-CEO of Hidden Compass, a media company celebrating nerds and modern-day exploration. As an award-winning travel and science journalist, Sabine has contributed stories to dozens of publications and been featured in exhibitions around the world. As an editor, she has managed content for travel companies valued at more than $500 million. As a Stanford-*

trained environmental researcher and community coordinator, she's worked on conservation projects from the Andean Plateau to the Great Barrier Reef. In 2009, she represented climate researchers at the United Nations. She's managed to survive dengue, the Peace Corps, an inadvertent partnership with cocaine-smugglers, and a mountain biking trip down 12,000 vertical feet of the world's deadliest road. Read more at www.sabinekbergmann.com.

PARENTING DANGEROUSLY

Diane Selkirk

Without warning, our boat made a sharp turn. Instead of riding down the eight-foot swells with the wind propelling us from behind, we were now pointing into the waves with the wind coming from ahead. It was as if we'd been skiing down a bunny hill and a rookie mistake caused us to face uphill and slide backward.

While the change in direction was uncomfortable, it was something that had happened before. Our ham radio, which allowed us contact with the world beyond our 40-foot catamaran *Ceilydh*, occasionally created electronic interference that disrupted our autopilot, causing wild 90-degree turns.

This time, my husband Evan was recording the locations and conditions aboard the dozen or so 'buddy boats' we were sailing in loose company with across the 2,800 miles from Puerto Vallarta, Mexico, to the Marquesas, French Polynesia, when our boat went wildly off course. So, as he kept speaking, I left our 9-year-old daughter Maia at the table with her boat schooling work and headed out on deck to fix things.

We'd been at sea for 16 days, and much of the morning's radio call was spent talking about where we'd all make landfall in 48 hours. Evan and the other boat crews debated the pros and cons of one island port over another (frangipani-scented jungle and towering fairytale mountain peaks versus tropical beaches and exotic villages). Meanwhile I spun the wheel and adjusted the sails, trying to get us back on course.

With growing confusion, I realized no matter what I did, the boat stayed facing into the liquid hills, shuddering with each wave impact, while the sails flapped uselessly.

"Something's wrong with our steering," I called to Evan.

He came to the cockpit and repeated my efforts and then joined me at the back of our boat.

Our rudders, which control the steering, are found on each hull's stern. "I can see this rudder," Evan said as he peered with me into the hypnotic blue depths, seeking out the rectangular shape, "but on the other side there must be an optical illusion, because I can't see that one."

"We can't see it because it isn't there," I said.

"Of course it's there," Evan said, who'd now leaned so far over the stern that the frothy sea licked at his hair. Worried he'd be swallowed by one of the bigger waves, I called Maia out for the tie-breaking decision.

"Definitely gone," she said after taking a quick look.

Shock was quickly replaced by action. By adjusting the sails and turning on the motor you can steer a catamaran with one rudder. While Evan began balancing our boat so one rudder could do the job of two, I reported our predicament to the other boats over the radio. Cautiously we got back underway and tried to pretend all was well.

I reassured Maia that losing a rudder was a manageable problem, and then to prove it I gave her some more schoolwork; French lessons and the geology of volcanoes.

With her busy, Evan and I looked over the charts and tried to pick the best harbour for our crippled boat (a town with skilled welders beat out tropical beaches and exotic villages) and sent out emails to alert the French Polynesian Coast Guard.

Always in the back of my mind as I checked schoolwork and made meals was the realization that our remaining rudder could be overpowered by a large wave and also break off. Occasionally the waves would knock our boat sideways and my heart lurched in cold fear. Having one rudder was stressful; but no rudders, hundreds of miles from shore, could lead to abandoning our boat.

The thought that ran through my head on a loop was, 'What kind of parent puts a kid in this sort of predicament?'

Evan and I met as teenagers at sailing instructor school in Vancouver, British Columbia. His plan was to design sailboats while sailing around the world; mine was to write about boats while sailing around the world. We made a good team. Within a few years we married and bought a cheap and sturdy little blue-and-white sailboat with round portholes and a swooping bowsprit. As her 20-something-year-old crew, we were the archetype of young adventurers.

Sailing is a wonderfully ancient and meandering way to travel the world. We'd slip into a new port at dawn and watch the land reveal itself. Practicing our Spanish, we'd be led to the market by giggling children then haggle over tomatoes with a shy woman who'd ask what snow felt like. In the evenings we'd sit at rickety tables, sharing bottles of tequila and our worldviews with people from every continent. With the idealism of youth, we were sailing toward a more deliberate life—one that just happened to include more risks than normal.

As a crew of two it was easy to choose adventure over caution. We surprised the locals when we arrived in a small village in El Salvador. We were the first cruising boat to enter port after the end of their civil war. Missing men, mortar-pocked buildings, and an overflowing prison contrasted with charismatic women who were determined to entice us to try the full range of local cuisine.

It wasn't the promise of sopa de pata (tripe soup), gallo en chicha (rooster in a fermented sauce) that saw us leave El Salvador and unwisely sail into a gale. Instead we left because we were in a hurry to get to Costa Rica for surf season. Our first night back at sea, when I was on watch and our little boat was being tossed on black waves, Evan was startled from sleep when our pressure cooker and a drawer of cutlery launched across the boat and smashed into the wall inches from his head.

Danger felt different before kids. The dented wall and other near misses became stories that were laughed and dramatized for other sailors over drinks. Settled life sounded like a shipwreck you couldn't sail away from.

Maia was born a couple of years later in an East Coast port thousands of miles from home. A year later we did what everyone expected and sold our little boat and headed home to Canada. We got good jobs and bought a home. But six years later we did the unexpected; we moved aboard a new boat and prepared to set off to see the world.

"Are you taking Maia? Pirates are so dangerous—can't you leave her here?" The question from a friend's sister was a familiar one. The implication was sailing as a young couple was an adventure but sailing as a family was reckless.

We'd met several cruising families while out sailing. It struck us as the perfect way to raise our future child—she'd have ready access to her parents and the world would be both her playground and school. But each time I tried to describe the wonders of sailing as a family it sounded irresponsible compared to their more practical concerns about pirates, illness, storms, and home schooling.

Sometimes I tried to explain how we'd thought it through; we'd weighed each risk and prepared for every eventuality. Even still it's a delicate balance to set sail with a child: Would our daughter be safe? Stay healthy? Could we replace her teachers and find her friends? And yet, we also were looking toward a horizon of unparalleled opportunity: raising a kid for whom the extraordinary becomes ordinary. Swimming with giant manta rays, international celebrations, friends from every continent—this would be the stuff of her childhood.

"She likes whales and being with us. And we'll avoid the regions with pirates," I had awkwardly responded.

Each day, each experience, slowly proved sailing was the best way for our family to live. One day, as we sailed toward an anchorage in the Sea of Cortez, I saw signs of a whale spouting on the horizon.

As I called Maia on deck to see, we saw more spray rising several feet in the air.

Then we spotted our first lumpy brown log-like shapes drifting across our path, each one sighing a fine, fetid mist. Taking in the bulbous heads and wrinkled skin, I puzzled over the species and then realized they were sperm whales.

While I did the identification, Maia was counting. "Forty! But that really big log might be two whales so maybe 41!" she called out as we made our way through the super pod, changing course every time another leviathan swam lazily into our path.

As they floated beside us, I tried to tell Maia the story of how the sperm whales had been hunted to near extinction for their oil. I wanted her to know the wonder of seeing a species come back from the brink of destruction. She missed the impromptu homeschooling lesson though, mesmerized by gazing into a whale's massive liquid eye.

As we sailed away from the final whales, rank whale breath still clinging to our sails, I wondered if I should have tried harder to get her to understand. Then I realized that maybe simply having to tack and change course over and over, just to work our way through an ocean thick with whales, was enough.

But on our voyage to the South Pacific on that first rudderless night, when the sun had set but the moon hadn't risen, when I was entering my 14th hour of trying to hide the kind of fear that constricts your breath and coats your skin like a bruise, sailing stopped feeling like a good way for our family to live.

Maia was in bed and Evan and I were outside under bright distant stars. "Maybe if we survive this," I said, "we could get a cabin in the mountains."

This, I realized, was what all those well-meaning questions from concerned friends and family had been about. At the time, I had been so confident that we were prepared for the challenges of sailing I hadn't taken into account the challenge of being a mother.

But suddenly it was apparent how little control we had over sailing and parenting. For all the things I wanted in that moment—

for the seas to be smaller, for our remaining rudder to stay strong—I also wanted to get to safety without my brave little sprite of a daughter absorbing my fear.

An endless feeling day later, our 18th at sea, I saw a smudge on the horizon. That's what land looks like when you first spot it from the sea. Over the course of an hour I kept my eye on it—watching it take form and hold—ruling out cloud and squall. When I was sure of what I was seeing, I called Maia and Evan out on deck. I pointed to the patch of dark gray outlined against a background of medium gray and held Maia's finger as I traced the shape. "The Marquesas!?" she whispered excitedly.

Then she whooped a "Land Ho!" When she looked at her dad, she saw he had tears in his eyes, "But we found it. Why are you crying?"

A friend told me that an ocean crossing is like childbirth; the moment you step foot on land, you forget the pain and fear of getting there. As we made our way into the harbour at Nuka Hiva, the largest of the Marquesas Islands, glimpsing the mountain peaks through the morning mist and absorbing the intensity of the tropical green, I realized I didn't want to forget our passage.

The first step ashore after crossing an ocean doesn't come with traditions the way crossing the equator does. Some sailors kneel and kiss the earth. But most, like us, just sway with land sickness and feel overwhelmed by the smell of flowers and overripe fruit, and the cacophony of birds, kids, and dogs.

What I wanted to do once we finished the formalities of checking in with the local authorities was to walk—to get as far from our boat as I could. So we climbed up through the heated jungle, legs shaking with the unfamiliar effort.

We were met on the trail by a Marquesan on horseback named Rue. He led us to a sacred site that was marked by huge banyan trees, sacrifice pits, and Tiki statues. Evan and I pondered the ruins of stone pyramids and platforms, while Maia and the kids from our buddy boats ran around picking mangoes, star fruit, and grapefruit from towering old trees. With fruit juice trickling down her freckled chin Maia exclaimed that she'd never eaten anything so good.

Everyone joked that this moment made the whole ocean-crossing thing worthwhile: standing in the sacred shade eating the best fruit in the world.

Breaking out of the jungle we reached jagged cliffs that jutted over the ocean. Maia looked out over islands that faded into the distance and asked which one we'd visit next. Evan and I looked back toward the harbour.

From our vantage we could see boats belonging to some of the boldest ordinary people in the world. *Ceilydh* jumped out at me. Sailing her was like riding a magic carpet into spectacular new world. She jumped out, not because she was most beautiful, but because it's hard to sail a boat across an ocean and not fall a bit in love with it.

Even if she did throw a rudder.

Reaching for my hand, Evan asked how I felt about the cabin in the woods. "We'll fix the rudder," he told me. "We'll solve each problem that comes up." Half-listening to Maia as she chattered about the adventures we'd promised and the things she wanted to see, I looked where she pointed. The islands were so beautiful, so mysterious; like a package on Christmas morning that was just waiting to be opened.

We were different from that young couple who set off fearlessly on their first grand adventure. When we sailed away from the Marquesas with our new rudder, I felt tentative and cautious. But a few days later, when we dropped our anchor in blue water of a remote Tuamotu atoll and I watched Maia confidently leap into the ocean to greet a manta ray, I knew that while our family had much to lose, we had an entire world to gain.

* * *

After spending much of the past decade circumnavigating the globe with her husband, daughter and Charlie the boat cat aboard a 40' sailboat, **Diane Selkirk** *has put her roots back down in Vancouver. She's continuing to travel but her focus has shifted to Canada and the US, and her work has expanded to include environmentalism and social justice. Her writing and photography for publications including* BBC Travel, Canadian Geographic, Cosmopolitan, Men's Journal, Pacific Standard, Saveur *and* The Globe and Mail *has been recognized with numerous awards.*

BIRDS, BUMPY TRAILS & BALANCE

Jenn Smith Nelson

I t used to be birds that brought us together.

Lately, though, spending time with my growing son, Finn, has become difficult. At nearly 12, he isn't as interested in watching birds with Mom as he is in playing with online friends on Fortnite, a game so addictive that the slow-natured pace of birding doesn't stand a chance.

Somehow, however, I convinced him to join me on a birdwatching trip along Canada's South Coast Birding Trail in Ontario. For four glorious days during the height of migration, we'd experience bird bliss in one of North America's premier birding destinations. I took it as an opportunity to reconnect with my growing-up-too-fast, moody-technology-obsessed-pre-teen, who was once joined at my hip.

To start, I should explain that the South Coast Birding Trail isn't an actual trail—rather, it's a network of hotspots that can be explored in various ways. Visitors can celebrate the arrival of all the spring avian visitors to Eastern Canada by hiking, biking, walking, or driving.

A few airplane stops from the prairies land us in Windsor, a city of 234,000 situated across the river from Detroit. We start at Ojibway Park, part of the Ojibway Prairie Complex. Spread out over 105 hectares (260 acres), the complex features diverse flora and fauna in natural areas that include wetlands, tallgrass savannah, prairie, and oak woodlands. An orchestra of sound hits us as we step out of the car and head toward the Nature Centre.

Once inside, we beeline to the floor-to-ceiling windows, where a variety of feeders hang on the opposite side of the glass. Attracting flashes of bright red, yellow, and orange, we are in awe as a Baltimore Oriole, several House Finches and goldfinches, a Yellow-bellied Sapsucker, and a Red-headed Woodpecker fly in to eat. A Downy Woodpecker, unafraid, eyeballs me through the glass only inches away.

Tom Preney, a naturalist at the Nature Centre who has been guiding at Ojibway for 15 years, greets us with a small Midland painted turtle in his hand. Finn is pretty excited by this, and others are excited by the turtles, too. The park is home to several turtle species, including endangered Blanding's, snapping, and Midland.

A Gray Catbird ducking in and out of the twigs of a fallen tree is the first bird I see as we start out on the Prairie Glade Trail, one of the park's four trails. "This trail will bring you through a mature Pinoche woodland," Tom says. "Some of the trees are 150- to 200-year-old, old-growth oak trees."

The smell of fresh rain fills the forest. "What's that noise?" Finn asks.

"That's a Blue Jay squawking," Tom answers.

The park is stunning with everything in full bloom. Mayapple plants that mimic little palm trees litter the forest floor alongside white-flowered woodland anemones.

Interested and curious, Finn asks all sorts of questions and Tom happily responds. Patient and passionate, between noting bird calls, Tom shares fun facts with Finn. Near a bridge, he points out a Blackburnian Warbler hanging out in the fork of a cottonwood tree. The warbler is followed by a Tufted Titmouse.

"That bird has a mohawk!" Finn says.

Tom scatters some seed, inviting the action to our level. Soon, two Red-bellied Woodpeckers, a White-breasted Nuthatch, and a Black-capped Chickadee swoop down. As they gobble the seed, we all hear a splash. Bumping against the side of the bridge, I have just sent our binoculars into the water. We recover them quickly, but day one has claimed its first victim.

Carrying on, birdsong competes with the high-pitched trills of American toads and croaks of western chorus frogs, making for a melodic musical backdrop.

"I hear a Blue-gray Gnatcatcher," Tom says, who calls it in with a "bshhh bshhh bshhh bshhh".

The gnatcatcher calls back as the zee zee zuzi zee song of a Black-throated Green Warbler nabs our attention.

I'm in heaven, but Finn has slowed down. Tired from the day, he complains his legs hurt, likely from recurring growing pains. A herd of white-tailed deer runs ahead of us as we finish up the rich nature experience at a pond where we find red-eared sliders, another turtle species.

Arriving at our accommodations for the night, the Holiday Beach Conservation Area, Finn sees his first Northern Cardinal.

"It's so red!" he exclaims.

A Wild Turkey, some Canada Geese, a scurry of eastern gray squirrels, and a fox also welcome us.

At the footsteps of the idyllic beach rental, which comes chock full of modern-day conveniences, is Lake Erie. Lured by the sight of waves through the window, I explore while Finn unwinds watching TV. Secluded with pockets of water and boardwalks, there are several great spots to look for birds, so I'm truly sad to leave the lovely area early the next morning.

As we pull away, light glows off the lake while drops drizzle down. Prepared, we've suited up for today's destination, Pelee Island. Part of a peninsula, it's a 90-minute ferry ride from the mainland. The island is a significant hotspot, thanks to its location at the crossroads of two major migration routes, and one of the first points of landing for spring migrants.

Looking at Finn, I can't help but grin at his new rain boots. They are enormous with nearly more boot than boy. Spinning wind turbines and solar panels dot entire fields as we weave along country roads. When we near the ferry crossing, we receive sad news that the ferry to Pelee Island has been cancelled due to wind gusts.

It's time to eat and regroup. Stopping in the town of Leamington, we devour a hearty breakfast at a bakery that doubles as a restaurant. Before I can even Google a new idea, Finn has acquired the Wi-Fi code and is engrossed in a Fortnite recap on YouTube. I let it slide as his mood, which was a bit sour from the early start, seems to be improving.

We decide on nearby Hillman Marsh. Adjacent to Lake Erie, the area features three miles of trails over 35 hectares (87 acres) of pristine marshland/shorebird habitat. There are several vantage points from within the brush and trees to open water and boardwalk. Making our way to the water's edge, Finn is pleased to spot a second cardinal singing happily from within the safe confines of a pine. A sense of pride that comes with the positive identification of what is quickly becoming his new favourite bird shines through.

The wind is blowing tall reeds to and fro as we amble along the waterfront, where busy Barn Swallows skim bugs off the water. There's a Killdeer a short distance away doing its best broken-wing impression. I explain to Finn how the act is a protective measure.

"He looks like a deformed pigeon!" Finn says, causing us to laugh loudly.

On a boardwalk over a small body of marshy water, Finn gets down on his belly trying to take a creative shot. His golden hair shines in the sun, matching the colour of the cattails, and it warms me to see him embrace the moment.

We trek through a woody patch following flitting warblers. Though we haven't been walking long, Finn begins to complain again, so I leave him at a bench to rest, and carry on. I pass a few Red-winged Blackbirds bathing in grassy puddles, and a pair of Yellow Warblers flash their sunshine sheens, swaying in harmony on branches. This time, they follow me from bush to bush. Immersed in trills, songs, and squawks, I feel happy and connected.

However, it's short lived.

"Mommmmmmmmm!" Finn shouts from the bench.

"Ten more minutes," I respond, frustrated.

I see his hands go up in the air as I continue the other way. He stomps away in true pre-teen fashion as I trek on a bit farther before begrudgingly moseying back to the car.

A short city break is needed, so we head to Kingsville, a town full of charming Victorian homes and delightful bird references. While walking along a quaint Main Street, we spot some chocolate birds in a window. Once inside Dutch Boys, we find precisely sculpted dessert birds and meet the two creative spirits who own the shop. Inspired by the area, Cor Boon, an award-winning wood carver, greets us and shares the process he and sculptor Henry Noestheden employ to create the decadent sculptures.

"This is an amazing part of the country that we live in," Cor exclaims.

En route to Point Pelee National Park, we stop for a quick bite at a double-decker "bustaurant" aptly named Birdie's Perch. Point Pelee, which is Canada's second-smallest national park, has been on my wish list for years.

It is an Important Bird Area and is on the UNESCO list of Wetlands of International Importance. The first national park in Canada established for conservation, it offers more biodiversity than any other national park and sees around 390 migrating bird species each year. As the southernmost point of mainland Canada, it's located at the same latitude as California (and Rome and Barcelona, too).

Spirits are high and the sun is shining as we enter the park. Finn beams when he sees the oTENTik—a raised-platform, tented A-frame structure that has everything we need to camp. Like he once did when he was small, Finn sets off exploring. Before turning in for the night, he insists on teaching me how to floss—no, not my teeth, rather the dance move made popular by … you guessed it, Fortnite. I comply and learn the dance, which garners hearty laughter. The good feels continue as we snuggle for the first time in ages.

I'm impressed when we get up early in the morning. It's day three and no words of complaint are murmured. It's a tad chilly, but we are hoping for a day of good sightings. After a birder's breakfast, we meet up with a group of 20 who've united for a two-hour Parks Canada-led hike, as part of the Festival of Birds.

"You see this bird here at three o'clock?" Bruce Di Labio, kicking off the hike, asks. "It's a rare species here—a House Sparrow! There are a few pairs in the park."

We learn quickly that Bruce, who has been birding here since 1974, is fond of bird jokes.

"But really folks, the bulk of the singing you hear right now is American Robins," he says, as we set out on the half-mile loop of the Tilden Woods Trail. Dutchman's breeches are in full bloom, their white petals reaching upward from the green forest floor along the trail sides.

Soon we hear more than robins.

The sweet shredded wheat of a Yellow Warbler and whitchity whitchity whitchity trills of a Common Yellowthroat ring through the cedar savannah and mature swamp forest.

"Oh, there it is," Bruce says, pointing to the yellowthroat.

Like a good tennis match, everyone turns their attention, all heads whipping upward in unison. Two French women attempting to get a look nearly knock over Finn, who is trying to photograph another cardinal.

Birding at this time of year, when the forest is near its densest, is best done by ear. So, it's great that Bruce is masterful with identifying the overlapping myriad of bird calls and songs. As the well-trodden trail morphs into a boardwalk, he shares every time he hears a bird, helping our lists quickly grow.

A pair of Swamp Sparrows, a Brown-headed Cowbird, a Baltimore Oriole, and a Ruby-crowned Kinglet all appear within seconds of each other. I attempt to get a shot of the kinglet, but the tiny speedster is too fast. The group flocks over the trail in a solid pack, all vying for glimpses.

It's a good mix of people of all ages and skill levels; nearly everyone has a giant lens, and many a competitive drive. Finn, however, is sticking close to Bruce, who is in front of the pack. Finn's impatience with being part of the large group is something we share.

We hear the descending chink chink chink call of a Northern Waterthrush as our group arrives at a swampy yet serene scene where cobwebs sparkle on still water. I spot Ontario's provincial flower, a white trillium, before we come upon another swampy area where a Swainson's Thrush appears.

Growing tired of the slow pace and ambitious attitudes, Finn walks ahead of the group. I realize maybe it's not my thing, either. Elbowing my way to the front is not my style, though I do appreciate the expertise of having such a knowledgeable leader. Feeling a bit claustrophobic, I trail behind for a bit. This, of course, results with me missing what would have been my first Blue-headed Vireo. I catch up just as a Scarlet Tanager is singing and posing for the bird paparazzi.

"It sounds like a robin with a sore throat," Bruce says, joking. Everyone chuckles. Suddenly, a wave of warblers takes centre stage and the park lives up to its coined designation as the "warbler capital of North America." First, a Yellow-rumped Warbler appears, followed by a Nashville, a Magnolia, and a magnificent Cerulean! All eyes are on the branches, and soon everyone is pointing and sharing sightings, leaving me more appreciative of the group effort.

The next day, we arrive at the last stop of the trip, Rondeau Provincial Park, for a small group hike.

"We've seen over 125 species the past few days, and over 20 warblers, including a Hooded and Kentucky warbler," Peter Simons, who is leading the hike, says.

Enjoying the hike's pace and camaraderie, we strike it rich with warblers again, spotting Chestnut-sided, Black-and-white, Black-throated Green, Prairie, and Orange-crowned warblers in the old-growth Carolinian forest. I finally get my Blue-headed Vireo, and a White-eyed Vireo, too.

While waiting for our flights home, I'm feeling grateful for the time spent reconnecting with my growing boy. Though it required a lot of give and take, I realize that, as much as my son enjoys spending time with me hiking and birdwatching, he wants it in smaller doses than I do. And because we are in an airport and not in a forest, I let it go and allow Fortnite to once again become his focus. Downtime comes in great varieties, after all.

* * *

Hailing from Saskatchewan, **Jenn Smith Nelson** *is a multi-award-winning freelance travel writer, photographer and new author. She's been published in four countries and in four languages, contributing hundreds of articles to 25+ outlets including* enRoute, Globe and Mail, Canadian Geographic, Toronto Star, Explore Magazine, Best Health Magazine, Nuvo, A Birder's Guide to Travel *and more. She also appears as a travel expert on CBC Saskatchewan's* The Morning Edition *and* Global News Morning Regina. *Jenn often writes about connecting with nature, wildlife, family and adventure travel. She co-authored her first book* 110 Nature Hot Spots in Manitoba and Saskatchewan *in April 2019. Find her online at travelandhappiness.com.*

BREAKING THE SEAL: TODDLER TRAVEL IN MAUI

Robin Esrock

I've cage dived with crocodiles, hung off the side of holy mountains in China, and raced horses in Mongolia. But here's the truth: The thought of travelling for the first time with my four-year-old daughter Raquel and nine-month-old son Galileo terrified me.

Curly-haired Raquel appears to have fallen Obelix-like into a cauldron of Red Bull. She's a spirited T4 bull in the China shop of my tranquillity. With a head yet to discover the stars, Galileo is newly teething, crawling, and addicted to wrapping his gums and baby carrot fingers around any hazard he can find. Sure, Raquel had already been across Canada, Brazil and New York, but it's different when they're babies, too young to put spiders in their mouths. It's different when there's two of them.

The sooner my kids learn to travel, the better, and so I thought I'd start somewhere easy: direct flight, warm, and with a range of family-friendly accommodation options. I often tell friends that expectations are the death of successful travel. It's no picnic on parenthood too. Before I got my hopes too high, it was important to acknowledge the facts: Children under the age of five are erratic, inefficient, agitated, annoying, moody, and masters of pushing buttons. Sure, you love them more than anything in the world, and there are moments of such tenderness, magic and wonder that you can't imagine life without them. But whether we're on the road or at home, no one can deny that we hard work for those moments, and pay for them in blood, sweat, tears, and dollars. Don't let anyone tell you otherwise.

No matter how great your toddler vacation is, the reality is it will be bookended by a flight one building over and three levels up from Hell. As a travel writer, I fly a lot. It's my chance to work, read, watch a movie, daydream at altitude. A six-hour flight from Vancouver to Maui should be nothing. If the kids sleep. Unfortunately, the only direct flight from Vancouver turned out to be a red eye. How bad could it be? Bad. Real bad.

Gali is licking tray tables and seatbelts. Raquel is having a full thermonuclear meltdown, vibrating with kicks and punches, and the plane is still at the gate. Rather than sleeping, they're using the seats and occasionally other passengers as a trampoline. Playing Frozen on the iPad subdues Raquel for a while, but it only worked once, and then she just, well … let it go.

Like condemned prisoners at a public hanging, my wife and I gaze into the eyes of fellow parents, dealing with the trauma of their own journey. Each minute of each hour has the weight of a cannonball. Frazzled by the experience, I commit a cardinal travel sin and forget our two bottles of duty-free liquor—our blessed late-night boozy escape—on the plane. I hastily run back to retrieve them, but Air Canada's cleaning staff relieved us of our bottles no more than five minutes after we had deplaned. "Sorry sir, our cleaners didn't find anything," the airline clerk says. Those fast-fingered cleaners must have young kids, too. I understand.

We grab our bags and shuttle to the car rental and spend the next forty-five minutes in a late-night line-up. Now the kids want to sleep. I push two chairs together and Raquel passes out. It's these simple hacks that make one a Parent of the Year. I eventually get our van, install the car seats, strap in the kids, and load the luggage. It's another forty-five-minute drive in the dark torrential rain to Wailea. Could anything be worth this?

Yes, waking up on the seventh floor in a Deluxe Ocean View suite at the Fairmont Kea Lani is definitely worth it. Sunlight sparkles off the Pacific below like a mirror-ball. Koi swim in ponds amidst manicured gardens and clear azure pools. Coconut trees rustle in warm tropical air with a fragrance sweet as nectar. Stripped of the jeans and hoodies we won't touch for two weeks, our family hums with travel buzz. We're chomping at the final bit of well-deserved beach vacation. When our feet touch the reddish sand of Polo Beach in triumph, it starts:

"I don't want to go to the sea, Daddy!" "Gali is eating sand!" "It's too hot, Daddy!" "It's too cold, Daddy!" "I'm hungry!" "I'm not hungry!" "Where's my blue spade?" "I want a red spade!" "I want what that other girl has!" "Pick me up!" "Put me down!" "This rock is scary!" "I want to go to the pool!"

Toddlers are complex algorithms dancing to a convoluted rhythm only they can hear. The first chance my wife and I get to relax is much later that night when both kids are asleep. No late-night walks on the beach for us, but we do sip cocktails on our lanai, beneath a planetarium of stars, the scene scored by the soporific sound of crashing waves. The flight is a distant memory. Aloha Maui. Finally, aloha.

Buffet breakfasts have ruined us. Raquel quickly gets used to having one mouthful of a dozen different dishes, and miso soup is now a breakfast staple. My wife and I tag team feeding both kids as Gali singlehandedly supports the birdlife of Hawaii gathering beneath our outdoor table to feed the snow of egg that falls from his highchair. Staff give us crayons for the kids each morning, and despite the buffet, Gali's favourite breakfast dish is Crayola Red.

Hours turn to days as we rotate between the pool, suite and beach. Raquel is too young for Kea Lani's Keiki Kids Club, but she can drop into its day-care-like facilities in the afternoon, when Gali is napping in the room and the sun is too strong. There were so many toys about I almost cried when we enter for the first time. Finally, she'll be happy, contained and entertained without me! Later, we explore the grounds, make a run to the nearest supermarket, and buy a few things we didn't pack while realizing we don't need most of the things we did. Later, the family dines at the sensational restaurant downstairs, a romantic meal of dreams invaded by our overtired, over-hungry kids who care little for the chef's inspired creations. Before the appies arrive, out come the apps. I survey the restaurant for looks of disapproval, but nobody makes eye contact, probably because they're afraid I'll ask them to look after the kids while I get a bite in. My wife turns to me and says: "Please don't go to the bathroom. I'm afraid you might run away."

Every time I meet a Dad or Mom in the knee high, pee-warm toddler pool where the kids spend most of their time (sandy beaches be damned), we share 1,000-yard stares, shrug our shoulders, and let the giggles and laughs of our kids melt our hearts. As with parenthood, it's so much easier to identify and share the challenges as opposed to the indescribable joys. There is an Adults Only section at the Kea Lani, and I wonder how many hearts are melting in it like ice in umbrella-topped cocktails. Travelling with young kids and travelling as adults would be comparing apples to oranges, both of which I recommend taking from the buffet in the morning because fruit comes in handy later for snacks.

Fairmont's luxurious resort was our high-end splurge, a refuge of stunning views that fluffed our eyes like pillows at turn down service. It is the other end of cheap. On our final morning, Galileo stands up in his hotel crib beaming his two-tooth smile and says "Dadda" for the first time. I pick him up, step out onto the balcony, and together we admire the postcard view before us. Cost of that moment: Priceless.

The most famous drive in Maui is the road to Hana, a hairpin-winding track alongside striking ocean cliffs. We made three turns and turned around, avoiding the projectile backseat vomit we knew would follow. This pretty much ruled out a drive to the Haleakala volcano crater too, but you have to leave something for future visits, with older kids. Instead we drive to Makena Beach, where Raquel flew a kite for the first time. I had brought it from home and since laying eyes on it she didn't want to do anything except fly that kite. Now! Please! Raquel flew the kite for exactly thirty-four seconds, and never wanted to see it again.

We drove up to Twin Falls and got some great photos amidst the giant bamboo and dual cascades, as well as the remarkable Banyan Tree in Lahaina with its sixteen trunks and a block-wide canopy. Raquel was having an allergic reaction to her all-natural sunblock, or the heat, or the seawater, or something the Internet told us could probably be treated with a little Benadryl. New parents would spend a day in a local hospital, only to be told to use a little Benadryl. Fortunately, we're over the nerves and constant worry that accompany the firstborn. Instead of rushing off to a hospital in paradise, we visit the island's famous Baby Beach, where the full-face snorkel mask I bought for Raquel is thoroughly enjoyed by all other kids on the beach. They tell me it works like a charm.

The full-face mask is the snorkel's first improvement in decades and allows the user to breathe and speak without anything in their mouths. I bought this one with ambitious plans to introduce my daughter to the wonders of marine life. This is why Raquel and I boarded Maui Dive Shop's Ali'i Nui catamaran in Ma'alaea Harbour for a three-hour snorkel expedition. Some strong winds derailed the planned sailing to Turtle Point, so we sailed up the coast to a protected reef. Raquel went bananas on the trampoline-like canopy at the fore of the ship, jumping around like a lunatic. She then ate a single piece of celery from the rib n' wings buffet. We suited up and hopped into the water with a kickboard, life vest and face mask. She looked down, and that was the end of my plan for viewing maritime wonders.

"I don't care if Humu the rainbow fish is dancing the cha-cha; I am not putting on that mask again!" Raquel has a way of saying all this with her eyes. To her credit, I did get her into the water a couple times, but she refused to look down. Advice for parents: If you plan on actually seeing or doing anything with your toddler, you're in for a disappointment. If you plan on just hanging out with your happy bouncing kid, it's smooth sailing all the way.

Further up the coast, about a half hour's drive from Wailea, is the second oldest hotel, and certainly the oldest-looking hotel, on the popular Kaanapali beach strip. The Kaanapali Beach Hotel bills itself as Maui's "most Hawaiian hotel," which means it is independently owned, has pioneered various cultural programs, and is far removed from the spit-polished gloss of the Fairmont. While the rooms look and feel like a throwback to the 1970's, the location is steps away from the beach, its whale-shaped pool a hit with the kids, and the well-kept gardens are full of native plumerias bursting with colour. Sure, the shower drain was blocked and the screen door unhinged, the bathroom tiny and the pillows a little lumpy, but the KBH is affordable, and as Raquel launched herself between the two beds, she yelled, "Daddy, this is even better than the last hotel!"

The needs of a toddler are tremendously simple: If you can jump on a bed, life is grand. Staff at the KBH were lovely and their KBH Aloha Passport kids program kept Raquel busy with hula and ukulele lessons. The on-site Luau performance and feast was fabulous, and it didn't take long for Raquel to get up on stage and participate. We could self-cater in the handy covered pavilion, and our oceanfront room was a few steps from the shallow break of Kaanapali's sandy beach.

Raquel quickly found a few friends, including a 5-year-old boy named Floran from The Hague, who she simply called "My boy!" They played for hours in the pool while his Dad and I made small talk and got sunburned. Gali awoke at 5:30 a.m. one morning and so I took him for a walk along the paved beach path, past the glitzy Whalers Mall and the Marriott and Hyatt mega resorts. There was a surprising amount of people on the trail. Many of them were pushing strollers. We aloha each other, sharing the camaraderie of young parent exhaustion with the elation of being in such a beautiful place at sunrise.

My wife deserved a break, and I wanted to treat her. Spas are the typical go-to, but massages tend to blend into each other, a short-term fix one forgets before the oil dries. Catching your first wave on a surfboard, however, is something you never forget. I looked after both kids while Ana took a surf lesson with Goofy Foot Surf School in Lahaina. She used to be a dancer so I figured her first lesson would be way more successful than my first lesson, which consisted of non-stop wipe-outs in the cold waters of Tofino, B.C.

With Galileo teething and up all night, I think Ana would have enjoyed two hours alone in a closet. As I entertained the kids onshore, she paddled out to a small break where all the surf schools gather. And there we watched her not only get up the first time, but stay up over and over again, graduating to a few bigger waves. She was as thrilled as I'd hoped she would be, immediately regretting that she'd waited so long to surf, considering she grew up on a beach in Rio. Nobody should ever say no to a massage, but if you want to treat your partner in Maui, give them a challenge to overcome in the healing waters of the ocean. And a break from the kids, of course.

By our third hop, we'd realized, as most travellers do, just how much we packed that we simply didn't need. We could blame the kids, but the reality is we can only blame ourselves. Having endured the worst Vancouver winter in years, we'd forgotten what warm weather feels like, that all we'd need is bathing suits and flip-flops (and diapers, wipes, toys, and stuffies). We packed up and headed north up the coast to the Napili Kai Beach Resort, framing a perfect crescent-shaped beach with toddler friendly waves.

Steps from the ocean is the resort's large pool, a hot tub, and a 27-hole putting green course Raquel couldn't get enough of. If you enjoy infinity pools like I do, you'll appreciate that Room 232 in Napili Kai's Puna Two building has an infinity patio. The view from the bedroom and kitchen is all ocean, so much so that it feels you're on a cruise ship. Meanwhile, the fully equipped modern kitchen quickly taught us this: If you're travelling with toddlers, a kitchen is gold. Oatmeal porridge at 3 pm? A cheese sandwich at midnight? No problem! Raquel helped me with the groceries for several nights of simple meals—spaghetti, oven fish, rotisserie chicken, and we saved a bundle. Importantly, the kitchen had a blender and icemaker to craft our own piña coladas.

After twelve days of sunshine, a tropical storm hit with sheets of raining falling for thirty-six hours. Confined to our room, we were relieved to be able to watch Netflix movies on TV (thanks to a handy HDMI cable connected to my laptop), stare at the ocean, and let Gali nap in his own space. Fortunately, there was still plenty of time to play on the beach, explore the grounds, bury Raquel in sand, make sandcastles, and splash in the pool. Tropical vacation bliss.

We're relaxed. We're finally in the flow, and on a schedule that works for the kids. Everything is great. Now let's dynamite that magic to hell. Air Canada's return flight from Maui is a red eye. (They don't call it Air Canada Rouge service for nothing.) We arrived at the airport two hours early and barely made check-in. Line-ups, heat, frustration, delays, wrong seat assignments—every hour that dripped by eroded the pleasant memories of Maui.

Once on the plane, the kids become caged monkeys, eventually collapsing in exhaustion on the unspoken condition that their parents would not. Ana bends herself into a pretzel on the floor with one kid using her as a pillow and the other as a footrest. Raquel has another epic meltdown on arrival, and by the time we get home, she climbs on the couch, puts a blanket over her head, and we don't hear from her for six hours. She's never done this before, and we really hope it's the start of a trend.

A few days later, the colours and tans of Maui are fading, but our experiences on the island remain bright, our photographs sealing in memories with a varnish that will only improve and become more valuable with time. I pick up Raquel from daycare, and ask her: "Did you tell everyone about Maui?"

"No," she replies. "I forgot to."

Toddlers.

She might be over it, but I'm hopeful our two weeks on the Valley Isle hardcoded our children with a love for the ocean, island life, the aloha spirit of Hawaii, and an appreciation for warm, sincere hospitality. It definitely hard-coded a love for travel, for the next sentence out of Raquel's mouth is: "Where are we going next?"

* * *

Robin Esrock (robinesrock.com) *is the bestselling author of* The Great Canadian Bucket List *and* The Great Global Bucket List. *Inspired by their experiences in Maui, the Esrocks decided to spend 12 months travelling in Australia and Southeast Asia.*

THE NIGHT THE SCORPION CAME TO DINNER

Grant Lawrence

After suffering through too many long, dark holiday seasons in rainy Vancouver, I was absolutely determined to somehow, some way, get my family out of town for the 2019 holiday break. Wherever we were going to go, it had to be cheaper than Hawaii, and it had to be someplace we've never been before.

After much hand wringing, second-guessing, and endless research, we finally decided upon a remote and moderately priced open-air jungle cabana nestled on the Osa Peninsula on the southwest coast of Costa Rica.

And we'd bring our kids, who were 6 and 3. Were we crazy? Maybe. But since those kids have been nature-tested repeatedly during summers in the coastal B.C. rainforest, we figured we were ready for the equatorial jungle.

Before the trip, we were intrigued to read that, for such a tiny country, Costa Rica is incredibly rich in biodiversity: It's home to 5% of planet's flora and fauna, including over 200 species of mammals, roughly half of which are bats. The area also offers over 225 different types of reptiles, more than 800 kinds of birds, and over 300,000 varieties of insects, many of which we would become intimately acquainted with during our ten-day jungle immersion.

The trip involved a complicated itinerary that took months to coordinate; direct flights from Vancouver to San Jose, then a transfer over to a much smaller plane that flew us down to the tiny outback fishing village of Puerto Jiménez. Upon arrival and in full, wide-eyed culture shock, we visited the local open-air grocery store to stock up for our journey.

The town buzzed with a rough and tumble mix of locals, surfers, eco-tourists and adventurers, many headed for the nearby Corcovado National Park, one of the best places on Earth to spot the elusive and endangered jaguar, as well as countless other jungle creatures large and small.

To finally find our cabana, we caught a ride in a hired jeep down a muddy dirt road over which several rivers flowed. The jeep splashed right on through those brown waters, much to my children's awe. After about ten hours of air travel and 45 minutes in the jarring jeep, we finally arrived at our steamy cabana, made almost entirely of bamboo, with the jungle surrounding us on three sides. We pulled in after dark to a cacophony of as yet unseen creatures.

A constant word of warning before our trip was to make sure we brought flashlights. In the tropics after sunset it gets dark very fast, like flicking off a light switch. The last thing you wanted to do was step on a venomous creature like a fer-de-lance pit viper, because it would indeed be the last thing you do.

We equipped our entire family with powerful headlamps before the journey, and they were the first things we reached for upon arrival. It was then that we realized that old-fashioned handheld flashlights would have been much less impactful than our headlamps.

As it happens, many nocturnal flying insects are attracted to light. Wearing a headlamp where it was intended to be worn, on my head, ensured that some of those 300,000 or so jungle bugs would end up on a wild collision course with my face. I realized this hazard the hard way during that first night, while illuminating the book I was reading to my kids with the headlamp.

Moths, beetles and other unknown tropical flying insects of all kinds repeatedly smacked into me. Putting the behemoth in moth, you know they're big when they come with horns. Many boasted bizarre, Transformers-like features. But it was a smaller, kamikaze-type moth that nailed me right in the eye. I instinctively closed my eye tightly and rubbed it, but my eye continued to feel irritated. Then it began to burn.

I rushed to the bathroom to wash my eye out. Upon closer inspection in the mirror, I saw something small, foreign, and moving. To my horror, I realized that it was a fluttering wing, sticking out from under my lower eyelid.

The wounded moth (coincidentally also my hockey goalie nickname) was still in my eye and still alive. I folded my lower eyelid down and carefully plucked out the twitching creature from my eyeball. It collected itself for a moment on the edge of the sink. Then it flew away.

The following morning at 5 a.m. my wife and I were startled awake under our mosquito netting by a chorus of deep, guttural roars coming from right outside the cabana. It was like nothing we had ever heard before, as if an army of angry orcs had descended upon us. We were petrified. Our kids slept through it.

It turned out to be what some refer to as the "rooster of the jungle," the howler monkey, which creates an echoing bellow that sounded as if it was coming from something much larger than their skinny 3-foot frames.

As our jungle vacation unfolded, we slowly became accustomed to the ever-moving world around us. One night, as we were sitting down to dinner, my son pointed to a pair of my wife's pants that were draped over a chair to dry, since everything in Costa Rica is generally humid and damp. My son shouted, "Dad! Watch out! It's a scorpion!"

One chair over from my six-year-old was an utterly uninvited dinner guest: Crawling slowly up my wife's pants was a large, black, and nasty-looking 4-inch scorpion, complete with its coiled, spiked tail and menacing front pincers.

After herding my family to the other side of the cabana, I grabbed a broom and carefully lifted the pants from the end that didn't contain the venomous arachnid, and proceeded to throw pants, broom, and scorpion out the window.

The next morning, I inspected the pants with the broomstick. They were scorpion-free. As I turned to deliver the news, my hairy legs were met by six more, attached to a fist-sized tarantula crawling slowly across our first step up to the cabana. I had to gingerly step over it to get back inside.

"Scorpion's gone but watch out for the tarantula at the bottom of the stairs."

After a few more days of insect and arachnid mania, we settled into the Costa Rica wilderness groove and found ourselves more often marvelling than recoiling. Whether it was the busy and extremely well-organized marching leaf ants on the ground, or the beak-heavy toucans that ate the nuts on the trees outside our cabana each morning, or the four species of monkeys—howler, spider, squirrel, and white faced—that swung from the treetops all day long, we realized that we were on a very special vacation. We even got used to the howler's morning reverie and were soon sleeping right through it.

We didn't even have to leave the cabana to catch the action. We could sit on the couch in the open-air living room and watch the wildlife show all day if we wanted. The spectacle was occasionally enlivened by odd-looking larger mammals that wandered out of the jungle. Like the coatimundi, a curious cross between an anteater and a raccoon with a long ringed tail that stands straight up, or a capybara, a guinea pig-like creature the size of a medium dog, and the largest rodent in the world.

Down on the beach, just a ten-minute walk from our jungle abode, we were delighted by colourful macaws, lounging iguanas, and ugly vultures. My kids loved chasing the sand crabs that raced sideways from hole to hole. The kids could also safely splash around in the bay's protected, shallow, and bath-warm saltwater.

Every day, we saw or discovered something new and awe-inspiring, like a fifty-foot waterfall deep in the jungle, or something that could kill us within seconds, like, say, the poison dart frog.

Despite the dangers, my wife and I realized that we might be reaching a new stage of parenthood where, if we saved properly, we could successfully take our children to other far off places full of adventure. Maybe Africa could be next? Or Iceland? The possibilities seemed limitless.

One of my favourite days during our jungle adventure involved a supply run back to Puerto Jiménez with my son. We caught a ride in the local zip line company's van and planned to catch the jungle bus back. In town we loaded up on groceries, beer, and, in preparation for my daughter's fourth birthday which we would memorably celebrate at the cabana, a few "birthday donuts" for lack of a cake.

We lugged the boxes of supplies out to the bus stop in the searing sun and waited. And waited. Finally, a pickup truck loaded down with people and supplies pulled up in a choking cloud of dust and exhaust fumes.

"Hombre!" shouted the driver. "You need a ride? No bus today, civic holiday!"

The interior of the pickup already looked jammed.

"Uhhh … well," I pondered.

"Dad?" my son asked incredulously, "are we … HITCH-HIKING?"

"Sort of, yeah," I replied. "Get in. And don't tell your mom."

Our groceries were tossed into the back of the pickup next to three bronzed, shirtless surfers with hair in their eyes and their boards at their backs. My son crawled into the backseat and I belted him up between two backpackers that looked and smelled like they hadn't seen a shower in weeks. No children's car seat to be seen. I hopped up front with the driver.

Stuffed tightly into that truck were a happy mix of people from around the world: The driver was originally from Costa Rica but had spent twenty years in New Jersey. The two backpackers beside my son were a couple from Australia and South Korea. The surfers in the back included a Brazilian, a Swiss, and a New

Zealander. The driver passed around cold bottles of Imperial beer. For the next 45 minutes, we exchanged happy, funny stories, a microcosm of humanity bouncing along the dirt road in a pickup truck.

And the first thing Josh did back at the cabana?

"MUM! WE HITCHHIKED!"

Looking back on it all now, we're deeply thankful that we took that chance to live amongst the pit vipers, scorpions, spiders, howlers, UFIs (unidentified flying insects), and the wonderful people of Costa Rica over spending another rainy December in Vancouver.

* * *

Grant Lawrence *is the host of the* CBC Music Top 20, *and the author of three bestselling memoirs:* Adventures In Solitude, The Lonely End of the Rink, *and* Dirty Windshields. *His first two titles won the Bill Duthie Booksellers Choice Award at the BC Book Prizes, marking the first time that the same author has won this prize twice. Grant Lawrence is also a Canadian Screen Award winner, the lead singer of the Smugglers, a columnist for the* North Shore News, *and the goalie for the Flying Vees beer league hockey team. He lives in Vancouver with his wife, singer-songwriter Jill Barber, and their two children. His goal is to visit one new place on Earth each year.*

SO I SLEPT IN ... A CAVE

Lavinia Spalding

From the back of our rented SUV, my four-year-old son, Ellis, asks, "Mommy, why are we driving through a river?" As water splashes the car, I explain: Our home for the next two nights is in a wild place, inaccessible to vehicles except via this rugged route, which, yes, involves driving through a creek—but Ellis isn't listening.

"Look at that mountain, Daddy! Can we climb it? Where are we? Are we there yet? Mommy, why are you driving so bumpy?"

This deluge of chatter isn't new; Ellis hasn't quit talking once during our drive along the Burr Trail Road, an old cattle trail turned scenic backway that slices through some of southern Utah's most jaw-dropping, and least touristed, terrain. He's shouted cheerful greetings to horses, compared enormous rock formations flanking the road to sandcastles and blocks of cheese, fired off colours of the landscape (orange, brown, purple, red, yellow, black), and—when the shoulder of the road became a canyon—squealed, "We're on top of the world!" My husband and I have flown our young son to a remote corner of the U.S. hoping to ignite in him a passion for wilderness, and our plan is already working. But it's about to get even wilder.

After emerging from the creek, we bounce along a thin dirt road, manoeuvring through puddles and swerving in a sandy patch (PSA: An all-wheel vehicle with decent clearance is required to access this property), until we reach our destination. I park by the horse corrals and for the first time, Ellis falls silent.

We are deep inside the Grand Staircase-Escalante National Monument, looking at our Airbnb for the night: a 5,700-square-foot cave blasted out of a 60-foot-tall, 150-foot-wide rock.

I've spent time in this monument before. Over a decade ago, I lived for several years in the nearby town of Boulder, population 250. I've also met our host, Grant Johnson, before. But even if I didn't know him, I'd have known of him. Grant is one of the region's most renowned wilderness experts, having guided backcountry trips for 22 years around the Escalante River, the last area in the lower 48 states to be explored and mapped.

We find Grant in the kitchen, canning salsa. There was a freeze a few nights ago, he explains, so he's hurrying to preserve the vegetables he harvested. When he moved onto the 40-acre property in 1977, it was nothing but rocks and sand dunes. Today the homestead has three huge gardens, more than 30 fruit trees, 20 acres of irrigated pasture, a swimming hole, three cows, six horses, three cats, one dog, and dozens of wild turkeys. Not to mention this cave, which is currently blowing our minds.

Grant gives us the tour. In each room is a massive glass-paned window that doubles as a door to endless wilderness. The living room features a large plate-steel woodstove and an oversized bean bag (which Ellis flings himself onto gleefully). Downstairs is the "jam room," where local musicians and guests who've brought instruments can play. A long wooden bridge leads to our wing, which includes two charming bedroom nooks, a lounge, and private bathroom. The floor is painted a cheerful blue, the furnishings are bright yellow and turquoise, and it's all unfussy and relaxed, which suits us perfectly; we've passed too many vacations fretting over the likelihood of our child destroying someone's pristine white sofa. Here, we have no worries. Or nearly none. As we tour the space, Grant answers our questions about the cave's creation, and Ellis starts climbing the walls. Literally.

In 1973, at age 17, Grant moved to Moab. At 19, he started putting himself through school by working with explosives in uranium mines. At 21, he ended up here, in Deer Creek, living in a tepee. Three years later, he purchased the forty-acre lot near the creek. When he met his now-former wife five years later, they moved into a bigger tepee, then a tiny trailer, where they raised their daughter. They spent 24 years without electricity, 17 of which they also had no hot running water or phone. "We weren't trying to be permanent campers," Grant explained. "We just couldn't figure out where to make a home." Finally, inspiration struck. He would blast a house into a rock: the giant Navajo Sandstone dome already on the property.

In 1995, Grant began dynamiting and, over eight winters, carved the cave with hundreds of blasts and thousands of individual drilled holes. Today, it's hydroelectric, with radiant heated concrete floors. A steel chimney is made of irrigation line, and a heat exchanger is MacGyvered from an old propane tank. The interior stays cool in summer and warm in winter. The project took approximately sixteen years to finish.

"I always told myself it was about the journey and not the end result," Grant says. "But the result is that it's so incredible to live here, every day I walk in and just go, whoa."

Listening to Grant talk, I realize he matches the landscape. His skin is the exact shade of sandstone, his hair resembles the streaks of white in the rocks, and his eyes are the blue desert sky. It's as if our host, having inhabited nature for nearly 45 years, has become nature.

As the sun begins to dip, Grant suggests we watch the sunset from the roof. We take his advice and lace up our hiking shoes. "We can climb the house?" Ellis asks, incredulous.

Before we go, I give him a primer: This is a sand dune that nature hardened over time. It's solid, but certain parts can still crumble beneath your feet. Ellis listens semi-carefully, then takes my hand and drags me uphill. The view from the top is spectacular. It's October, and yellow cottonwood leaves glimmer against cinnamon-coloured buttes. On the descent, I teach him to side-step on the slickrock. He insists on practicing by climbing up and down three more times before dinner.

We brought food and could have cooked in Grant's well-outfitted kitchen, but instead we drive twenty minutes into tiny, remote Boulder—the last incorporated town in the continental U.S. to receive its mail by mule train—where my sister owns a farm-to-table restaurant called Hell's Backbone Grill. We sip craft cocktails, eat elk stew, and inhale dark gingerbread with butterscotch sauce. When we return to the cave, the night is black as iron, and the stars, in contrast, like neon. We stare up, and the sky stares back. It's vast, so much bigger than usual, all its edges stretched. Standing together in the dark, I can hear nothing except our collective breath. We are deeply isolated, and closer than ever.

Early the next morning, we snuggle in our comfy queen bed and gaze out the window as dawn turns the cliffs twelve shades of amber. Following breakfast and several cups of Grant's strong coffee, we wander out to explore. While weaving up the cliffs, Ellis notices the cave below. "I can see our house from here!" he yells.

I'm determined to teach him all I can about this place. He already knows a dozen new dinosaurs have been unearthed in the monument since 1998. Next is a lesson on cryptobiotic soil, the black moss-like living organisms that protect the ground from erosion while feeding it nitrogen and carbon; they're fragile as brittle leaves, I explain. Armed with this new knowledge, he becomes a desert defender, vigilant about our every step.

I pull a sprig of sagebrush for Ellis to smell, and a juniper berry he can nibble. We show him wild animal tracks and ironstone concretions, cacti and tiny wildflowers. And when he lies down on the ground and starts sifting fine red sand through his fingers, I enjoy a moment of pure parental relief. He's forgotten, at least temporarily, about Legos and YouTube cartoons.

I'm excited to find a lithic, the scrap of an arrowhead (but not surprised; the monument has been inhabited for 13,000 years) and explain why we need to leave it behind: because a monument belongs to everyone. It's a place for all to enjoy, respect, and preserve. What I don't say is that this particular monument was recently reduced by nearly 50 percent and divided into smaller chunks, a decision made by the administration to open it to mining and drilling. What I don't say is we've brought Ellis to this land we love so he'll love it, too, and grow up fighting to protect it.

Back in the cave, we spend our afternoon showering, napping, taking photos, reading, and enjoying the profound quiet. At dusk, we wander outside to join Grant, where he's roasting poblano peppers, slowly turning the crank of a metal basket filled with red-hot coals and peppers. The air is dust and spice, a quintessential Utah recipe.

Grant tells us he considers this an adventure house. "You're at the center of the monument," he says, "so you just get up in the morning and go. If you see something cool, you stop and check it out. When you discover a special spot, even if a million people have been there before, it's yours."

The next day, we follow his advice: Get up in the morning and go—back through Deer Creek, down the Burr Trail, past pale domes, buttery cliffs, maroon hoodoos, a slot canyon. When we pull over to hike and Ellis shoots straight up the sloped slickrock, I feign composure. This land is beautiful but brutal, and I'm silently freaking out about him slipping and hitting his head. I'm also keenly attuned to the importance of encouraging his independence. I stop myself from calling out, warning him to be careful. Instead, I stand back and admire my son's newfound confidence. Though he's spent only a few days exploring this unfamiliar terrain, he deftly scrambles up and sidesteps down. He's tanned and dusted with red dirt, his hair messy and sun-streaked, his pockets full of rocks. He's thoroughly immersed and is now our teacher, showing us that in a place like this, it doesn't take long to become nature.

This essay was first published in Airbnb Magazine *November 2019. Republished with permission.*

* * *

Lavinia Spalding *is series editor of* The Best Women's Travel Writing, *author of* Writing Away, *and co-author of* With a Measure of Grace *and* This Immeasurable Place. *She introduced the e-book edition of Edith Wharton's classic travelogue,* A Motor-Flight Through France, *and has contributed to such publications as* AFAR, Longreads, Tin House, Yoga Journal, Sunset, Airbnb Magazine, Ms., Post Road, The San Francisco Chronicle, The Guardian, *and* The Best Travel Writing. *She has won gold Lowell Thomas and Solas awards, and her work has been recognized in* The Best American Travel Writing. *When she isn't teaching writing workshops around the world, Lavinia lives in New Orleans and on Cape Cod with her family. Visit her at laviniaspalding.com.*

BLAME IT ON THE BEARS

Lucas Aykroyd

"Look at the bear playing hockey!" I exclaimed, pointing to the colourful banner outside the Leningrad Ice Circus. For a 10-year-old Canadian boy, this cartoon, depicting a relative of the 1980 Moscow Olympic mascot Misha with a hockey stick and skates, really had it all.

"That's funny!" my dad said. My mom and my six-year-old sister Clarissa chuckled too. Our tour group was lining up with Russians in dark coats to enter the round, 3,000-capacity circus. And in the pre-Internet era, we didn't realize what lay ahead.

Where do you take your pre-teen kids on their summer vacation in 1985? The Soviet Union, obviously.

Our family, who lived in Victoria, British Columbia, had a geographical advantage. Every summer, we flew—usually from Seattle to Helsinki—to visit my maternal grandmother for three or four weeks in Turku, Finland's oldest city. Often, we checked out a nearby country as well.

In 1984, we visited the original Legoland in Billund, Denmark, sporting garbage-bag raincoats on a drizzly day as we admired a Lego diorama of ancient Egypt. The following year, my dad took things up a notch by booking a five-day round-trip tour of Leningrad (now St. Petersburg). For the four of us, it cost about $600 CAD for the bus trip, hotel, food, guides, and admissions to attractions. I was thrilled, and not because of the price tag.

At age six, my first big international hockey memory was watching the USSR slaughter a Wayne Gretzky-led Team Canada 8-1 in the 1981 Canada Cup final. When I was seven, I devoured my parents' paperback edition of *Animal Farm*, George Orwell's dark parable of Stalinist repression. And after the Soviet military shot down Korean Air Lines Flight 007 in 1983, I was horrified to read the news in the *Victoria Times-Colonist*, given all the long Finnair flights we took.

For almost any kid living in the Western world in the 1980's, the Soviet Union loomed large in the imagination—just larger than average in mine. The Cold War was still in full force, with talk of nuclear missiles on the news most nights, and Mikhail Gorbachev was "the new guy." It felt like anything could happen.

It was about 380 kilometres from Helsinki to Leningrad. The bus ride to the Russian border felt significantly longer due to a group of young Finnish guys who weren't looking for a cultural experience. Even though cheap Communist vodka was just a few hours away, they'd already been drinking. We had to pull over because one of them had overdone it.

Getting into the Soviet Union was not easy. (Never mind the arcane pre-trip visa applications.) The KGB border guards searched everyone's bags. A long line of German tour buses—with apparently two gigantic suitcases per passenger—made the process even more tedious.

In terms of reading material, you didn't want to get caught with *Animal Farm*, the Bible, or anything else that could be deemed anti-Soviet propaganda. An officer with green shoulder boards carefully inspected *Martin Eden*, the 1909 Jack London novel my dad had brought along. He handed it back with a nod after observing that this book, describing a young proletarian writer's struggles, was actually on the officially approved list.

My mom had told us, "Russians are fond of children." The message had definitely sunk in. I repeated that sentiment several times to Clarissa before we arrived. She was too short for the immigration officer to see while checking our passports, so my dad held up her up, and the officer cracked a smile.

Less than an hour away, we stopped for a bathroom break in Vyborg, a former Finnish town on the Baltic Sea that the Red Army captured in 1944. A huge blood-red portrait of Lenin overlooked the main square. I gaped at the Bolshevik leader before heading into a pitch-black room with a trough. The neat, white-tiled serenity of Finland felt far away.

Arriving in Leningrad that evening, we checked into the Hotel Evropeiskaya. Just off central Nevsky Prospekt, the 1875-built hotel has welcomed illustrious guests from Pyotr Tchaikovsky to H.G. Wells. Rebranded today as the Belmond Grand Hotel Europe, it wasn't quite as swanky in 1985.

When you're a kid, you always remember the bathroom bloopers. So, just as I was delighted when our toilet at Vancouver's Hotel Georgia let out a loud burping noise in 1983, here I was startled when I tried to turn on the water in the bathroom sink.

"Mom! The tap came off in my hand." Welcome to Russia.

Downstairs at the Beriozka, the Soviet souvenir store was reserved for tourists with Western hard currency. We bought a Matryoshka nesting doll and an English-language version of *The Adventures of Captain Wrungel*, a 1937 children's classic by Andrei Nekrasov. I realized that communism had certain advantages when the clerk gave my dad his change in the form of Danish chewing gum. Yum!

The Soviets liked to keep things red and slightly overheated indoors. This philosophy extended from our hotel room to the breakfast buffet room, which featured red velvet walls. The breakfast menu was familiar. After our frequent trips to Scandinavia, Clarissa and I weren't fazed by the salty fish, yogurt, and cucumbers adorning the buffet table.

However, the big pitchers of kvass were different. Kvass, a refreshing, lightly fermented drink made with rye bread, was ubiquitous in the USSR. To my 10-year-old palate, it wasn't that different from apple juice. We guzzled it with glee. The hungover Finnish guys always stumbled in to refuel just before the buffet shut down.

Clarissa and I weren't allowed to drink kvass from the vending machines on Nevsky Prospekt. The machines had stacks of dirty cups that anyone could use. We noticed Russian mothers pulling clean cups out of their bags for their kids.

With the Soviet economy sputtering, there were long line-ups outside the stores. One day, I was surprised to see everyone coming out of a Nevsky Prospekt grocery store with string bags full of apricots. I hadn't had my growth spurt yet, but even though I was in Peter the Great's "Venice of the North," a 1703-built port city of palaces and canals, food and drink were always on my mind.

So when our Intourist guide took us around the State Hermitage Museum, the world's second-largest museum after the Louvre at nearly 67,000 square feet, I didn't moan about all the walking, since I was a proud member of the South Park Elementary School cross-country team. I was captivated by the ornate green pillars and fireplace in the 1839-designed Malachite Room, one of the showpieces in the Winter Palace, which was home to the tsars until the 1917 Russian Revolution. And even though I would have preferred to see a famous Leonardo da Vinci painting that wasn't a *Madonna and Child*, it was still Leonardo and therefore cool. But I did get hungry.

Alas, the cafeteria lunch line-up was not cool. In a bizarre display of bureaucracy, the Hermitage filled the cafeteria to capacity and then shut the doors. Nobody else was allowed in until the entire preceding group had finished eating and departed. I realized that Communism had certain disadvantages.

Were we bugged and followed in Leningrad? Possibly. Oleg Kalugin, a former KGB major general who defected to the West, revealed in a 1994 book that the Hotel Evropeiskaya had hidden microphones in certain rooms and that almost all Intourist guides were KGB informers. Still, our family had no nuclear secrets to spill.

We gabbed about the tasty ice cream and the Cyrillic characters on the Pepsi-Cola bottles—Pepsi had outmanoeuvred Coke for exclusive distribution rights in the Soviet Union. We laughed about getting sprayed by the fountains at Peter the Great's Summer Palace, which we visited by hydrofoil on the Neva River. That was sophisticated transportation. I can still see the clunky Soviet cars—surprisingly few for a city of five million—trundling along Nevsky Prospekt on the June "white nights."

Still, no other sight could top the Leningrad Ice Circus's hockey-playing bears.

Clowns skated around. Trapeze artists swung and flipped over the rink. "Kalinka"-style music got the audience clapping along. It was fantastic, but apart from the ice factor, it wasn't overwhelmingly different from the Shriners Circus that visited Victoria's Memorial Arena each year. That is, until the bears came skating out with hockey sticks.

I gasped. "Are those real bears?"

At first, we thought they were actors in furry suits, even though they moved rather awkwardly for humans. Hockey nets were set up and the referee dropped the puck. One bear tripped the referee, got a penalty, and skated off to the penalty box. When another bear crouched down and tried to gnaw at the puck, it became undeniable.

"I think they are real!" my dad exclaimed.

Several Russians sitting in front of us, presumably having heard variations on this conversation before, turned around, nodding and gesturing. Yep. Real bears.

The evidence still exists on YouTube. Today, I can't defend what must have gone into training the bears to play hockey. In 1985, I'm not sure it even crossed my mind. At the circus in Victoria, I'd joined other kids to ride an elephant, swaying high above the arena floor. Our city council wouldn't vote to ban circus acts with animals until 1991.

Looking back, those Leningrad bears encapsulate what made the Soviet Union a magical and sinister place for me. And our family never quite got it out of our system.

Clarissa has taken Russian lessons. She acquired an insatiable thirst for spy novels, attending John Le Carré's book launches in London, where she now works in publishing. Meanwhile, as a hockey journalist, I've just kept on going back to post-Soviet Russia, with a generous serving of déjà vu.

In 2000, I returned to St. Petersburg as the editor of the International Ice Hockey Federation's first-ever official World Championship web site. After the host nation's opening 8-1 win over France, I spotted newly installed Russian leader Vladimir Putin across the room at a reception, flanked by his gigantic bodyguards. The metaphorical bears proved toothless, as the Russian team collapsed and finished in eleventh place.

In 2014, I gaped at the massive menace of Bely Mishka, the polar bear mascot of the Winter Olympics, during the opening ceremonies in Sochi. Between hockey games, I visited Stalin's summer home.

In 2018, I turned down invitations to cover the Commonwealth Games in Australia and the Rock and Roll Hall of Fame inductions in Cleveland. I was unavailable because I'd already committed to a junior hockey tournament in Magnitogorsk and Chelyabinsk. Those industrial cities in the Ural Mountains supplied steel, ammunition, and tanks during World War II.

You get the picture. I'm now older than my dad was when our family went to Leningrad. It's weird when I think about it.

How did I go from lining up for goalie Vladislav Tretiak's autograph in Victoria to leading a panel discussion that included the now-president of the Russian Ice Hockey Federation at an international summit in Copenhagen? In my leisure time, what compels me to re-read Archie Brown's *The Rise & Fall of Communism*? Why do I own a teddy bear-shaped honey jar from the Republic of Bashkortostan?

Blame it on the bears.

* * *

Lucas Aykroyd is an award-winning travel and hockey writer based in Vancouver. His work has appeared in the New York Times, *the* Washington Post, *and* National Geographic. *Since 1985, he has visited the former Soviet Union 14 times, including the 2014 Olympics in Sochi and four IIHF World Hockey Championships in Moscow and St. Petersburg. Note: Lucas cannot guarantee that drinking fermented horse milk in Ufa or discovering how the KGB bugged the Hotel Viru in Tallinn will be fun for the whole family.*

YOU MUST REMEMBER THIS

Olivia Stren

I have landed in the pages of an F. Scott Fitzgerald novel.

That thought hits me as we pull up to our hotel in Casablanca. One of this Moroccan city's newest lodgings, the Hôtel and Spa Le Doge occupies a 1930s mansion. Each of its suites is named and individually designed to honour a leading figure of the art deco epoch—Fitzgerald, Colette, Coco Chanel, Jean Cocteau. The bellhop escorts my mother and me up a winding, crimson-carpeted staircase and leads us to the Fritz Lang room, named for the director of the 1927 movie *Metropolis* and aptly adorned with cinema-style tripod floor lamps and walls painted a smart, filmstrip gray. The bellhop deposits our luggage, then turns toward my mother and, apropos of nothing, says: "Vous avez le ciel et la lumière du Maroc dans les yeux, madame—You have the sky and the light of Morocco in your eyes, madam." My mother, her sky-and-light eyes now tearful, brings her hand to her chest and responds: "Je suis Casablancaise. Et j'ai le Maroc dans mon coeur, monsieur—I am from Casablanca, and I have Morocco in my heart, sir."

Claude Stren, née Schétrit—my mother—was born in a taxicab in Casablanca in 1941, a year before the classic film *Casablanca* was released. To me, her early life seemed like a movie: glamorous in its tumult. If Humphrey Bogart and Ingrid Bergman's *Casablanca*— filmed in studios in Burbank, California—was about longing and loss, my mother's Casablanca was too. Her Morocco, a country she was forced to abandon for political and religious reasons more than 50 years ago and has longed for ever since, instilled in me a yearning for a grander, more operatic life.

I was born the boring way, in a hospital, and grew up in safe, comfortable Toronto, with its grumpy, overcast skies, hearing about my mother's native city—its slicing light, its Ajax white buildings, its temperamental, wind-tousled Atlantic shores. For as long as I can remember, my mother and I talked about an idyllic someday when we would visit Casablanca. But she feared she would be returning to an unrecognizable city. So we let Casablanca flourish in the haze of fantasy—until my mom celebrated her big 70th birthday in 2011, and we finally booked the airline tickets.

"I am afraid of confronting the work of time," she admits to me somewhere above the Atlantic Ocean on the plane flight over. I do not tell her this, but I am feeling nervous too, that our high expectations will lead only to a letdown.

Standing on our hotel's rooftop terrace, we see Casablanca spread before us: 1930s-style town houses crowned with tropical gardens filled with lemon trees and trees that locals call filles de l'air (girls of the air), minarets pointing up to preposterously blue Moroccan skies the likes of which inspired Henri Matisse. But we also see grime-veiled apartment blocks with Berber rugs dangling over rust-scabbed balconies.

When the French established a protectorate in Morocco in 1912, they saw an opportunity for Casablanca to become the pinnacle of colonial achievement: a brand-new seaside fantasia of art deco and neo-Moorish architecture. Paris with palm trees. But the colonial government gave way to independence in 1956, and today Casablanca has a determinedly different character. Redolent of Havana or Buenos Aires, Morocco's most populous city has a splendour of bygone days.

Travellers in search of a mystical, snake-charming Morocco tend to relegate Casablanca to a night on the itinerary—a stopover en route to the imperial cities of Marrakech and Fès. Locals also sometimes deride Casa, as it's nicknamed, as a traffic-choked financial center.

But Casablanca native and Hôtel Le Doge owner Mounir Kouhen is one of a growing number of Moroccans who are committed to rehabilitating the city's reputation and architecture. He joins us on the rooftop, immaculately outfitted in a charcoal gray suit and pink tie. "We wanted to bring back Casablanca's artistic universe, its golden age," he says. "We took three years to renovate this building and quickly found its soul, its heart. Now it's ours to protect." He then adds, "Casa is different from other Moroccan cities. It spills over with energy." The sounds of horns interrupt him as if on cue. "This is the New York City of Morocco. But something that people may not know is that Casa is also a city beloved of Jacques Brel, of Édith Piaf."

"That is my Casa," my mother says. "That's the only one I know."

In search of Brel's and Piaf's Casa, we head to Villa Zévaco, in the city's chic Anfa district. Designed circa 1950 by the French-Moroccan architect Jean-François Zévaco, the villa gleams with white curving balconies and opens to a garden. Though it now houses Paul, a French pastry chain, the building seems the kind of glamorous retreat Piaf might have been drawn to during the times she spent in Casablanca to be with the love of her life, Algerian prizefighter Marcel Cerdan. Cerdan died in a plane crash in October 1949. About their love, Piaf composed the lyrics to her great warhorse song, "Hymne à l'Amour."

We ask for a coveted seat on the vast outdoor patio—the city's bourgeois brunch hub—which is decorated with wild palms and succulents. Morning sunshine filters through a tangle of silvery olive trees. Next to us, women with oversize sunglasses, designer purses, and French manicures compulsively check their BlackBerrys, while men in Adidas tracksuits and slicked hair sip mint tea and fidget with their iPads. I take a peek inside: waiters in white caps glide along black marble floors ferrying trays of toasted baguettes, olive oil, and honey.

Inspired by the beauty of the modernist Zévaco building, I suggest a visit to the city's so-called art deco district.

"I have never heard of such a place," my mother comments, poorly concealing her irritation—as though its unfamiliarity, much like the women and their giant eyewear, was an act of betrayal, another way the city and its people have gotten along just fine without her.

"I'd be happy to explore that area," she says, "but first I need to find my apartment building. My neighbourhood. If I don't find that building, I won't function."

So we hail a taxi to her old neighbourhood. Or at least we attempt to hail one. After about 15 minutes of strategizing, staking out different street corners—Kouhen's Manhattan analogy is apt—we are triumphant and are taken on a harrowing ride to the city's core.

If this is my mother's childhood stomping ground and the former center of la nouvelle ville, it's also, we quickly learn, the art deco district. "I lived in the heart of the art deco district without even knowing it!" my mother says, cheered by the discovery.

"I guess it wasn't called that when you lived here," I say, stating the obvious.

"No. It was just my neighbourhood. It was beautiful, but I didn't think it was special; I thought the whole world looked like this," she answers as we pass Au Petit Poucet, a café where the French writer Antoine de Saint-Exupéry came for coffee. An aviator as well as a writer, Saint-Exupéry stopped regularly in Casablanca in the 1920s between flights across the Sahara to Dakar, Senegal.

The café reminds my mom of one of her favourite Saint-Exupéry quotes: Je suis de mon enfance comme d'un pays—I am from my childhood as from a country.

"He also said something like 'Childhood is a place, a republic,'" she adds. Then she says, "To me, not finding the country of your childhood is, in some ways, not finding your home or yourself."

"We'll find it," I reassure her.

The capital of her childhood country is the Boulevard de Paris, where she lived. "It was an address of 'grand standing,'" my mother tells me, becoming the proud little girl. However, her family was far from wealthy (as a child, she suffered from rickets, a result of malnutrition), so she and her parents and sister made do in a tiny apartment in the back of a fashionable apartment building. On this Boulevard de Paris—once trimmed with café terraces and markets selling jambon-et-saucisson (ham and sausages)—young Claude dreamed of visiting the real Paris.

"I imagined it would be like Casablanca—sunny and beautiful— but with lovers sitting on benches and children sending paper boats to float in the Tuileries Garden." When she finally did visit Paris, with its iron skies and stubborn drizzle, she was disappointed. "I thought Paris would be paradise! Instead, in many ways, in Casablanca I had paradise under my nose."

Soon we come upon the Boulevard de Paris, hoping to discover at least one corner of that paradise. But it is grand only in recollection.

"This cannot be the boulevard!" my mother exclaims to me, almost angrily. "It's so small. The street is so narrow. It looks as if it was made for elves. And it used to be so immaculate!"

Buildings once painted in sharp blues and whites now are dirty, peeling, some in a state of literal collapse. We walk up and down the block three times. My mother seems disoriented, unable to find any signposts of her former life. I begin to wonder if this trip was a mistake—recover-the-past rarely makes for a winning travel plan.

Then she looks up and gasps "Pharmacie Minuit!" This pharmacy was just steps from where she lived.

"The apartment must be here. I know it's here." She's right. A few steps away stands her building, but renumbered, scruffy, the color of car exhaust. We step into this tiny province of her childhood.

"Do you recognize it?" I ask her.

"Yes, but it used to be cared for," she says.

The building's inner courtyard, once lush with ivy, is bare, and flower beds, once tidy green quilts, are covered in concrete, making them look like children's tombstones.

"I remember standing in that corner of the courtyard," she tells me, pointing, "with my sister and parents during the war," referring to World War II. "We were afraid that if we stayed in our apartment the ceilings would collapse, so we huddled together trying to find safety from the bombardments. The sound of the breeze in the ivy scared me, but I pretended it didn't. I wanted to be brave." My mother was three, and if she barely knew her name, the Nazi-leaning Vichy government, she recalls, knew it, putting hers (along with the rest of her family's) on the lists of those bound for Nazi concentration camps. Then, the Americans docked in Casablanca.

"I still recall the sound of champagne popping," she says of that happy night. "Uniformed soldiers, tall and handsome, gave us toy tanks and bars of Hershey's chocolate." She pauses, then adds, "And Lewis from Chicago, a soldier who was billeted with us, fell madly in love with my mother. Everybody did. She was beautiful."

In that night's delirium of relief and jubilation, my mother says, Lewis swept her up in his arms so she might touch the ceiling with her dimpled hand. In that little moment she felt joy was boundless. But today, we hear only the hollow sound of pigeons flapping overhead.

"All I see now is what I do not see," she says sadly, of Lewis, of her mother and father, of the neighbour she called Tata (for aunt), who taught her how to cook the fluffy couscous that made its way to our dinner table in Toronto.

Later that afternoon, her mood lifts as we play tourist and visit the spectacular Hassan II Mosque. Built on a promontory in homage to a Koranic verse stating that Allah's throne was built upon water, the mosque was commissioned by the late King Hassan II and inaugurated in 1993. Its 689-foot-high minaret is the tallest in the world and is bejewelled in tiles the colours of emeralds, sapphires, and tourmalines. We wander past fountains and under marble arches, then spot the El Hank lighthouse, just to the west along the shore. It is as plain in looks as the minaret is magnificent, but its ordinariness emanates a grandeur—of one that has witnessed and survived. It is the lighthouse that guided the Allies to Casablanca's shores.

"Unlike me, it hasn't changed. Not a wrinkle," my mother says as we sit atop the seawall, the waves below tossing themselves against rocky outcrops. "That lighthouse saved my life."

We return the following day for a deeper look at the art deco district, on a tour led by Florence Michel-Guilluy, an art historian who has lived in Casablanca for the past five years and now works with Casamémoire, a non-profit heritage-preservation association. "Casa is an architectural laboratory set under an open sky," she says. "The remarkable thing is not only the diversity of the building styles but their coherence. Casablanca is a city that one must explore le nez en l'air"—nose in the air, looking up.

So, nez en l'air, we wander past the Cathédrale du Sacré Coeur, a confection white as whipped cream that was built in the 1930s. "What made Casablanca modern was the way it celebrated tradition," says Michel-Guilluy, noting the minaret-inspired steeples.

As we walk onto broad Place Mohammed V, Michel-Guilluy notes, "The best examples of Casablanca's golden age are found here." We stroll over to the adjacent Parc de la Ligue Arabe, lined with towering date palms, where my mother and her mother walked. Hemming the park are the city's main post office, built in 1918, with all the arches and vibrant mosaics of a Moorish palace, and the imposing Banque al-Maghrib, with its elaborately carved front. More arresting to me, however, are the details that dress ordinary apartment buildings here: seashells carved into stone façades, Italianate balconies, green-and-gilt peacocks decorating wrought iron doors.

Anita Leurent, who recently moved from France to Casablanca, has joined our tour.

"In Casa, beauty is not served up to you as it is in other places. You must seek it out. Here, you are a treasure hunter, a chercheur d'or—gold seeker. That is what is thrilling!"

We pause at a 1930s town house, windows framed with plasterwork as delicate as lace. "There is always a detail, a secret to discover here," says Michel-Guilluy.

In the meantime, I am also discovering family lore. As we walk down Boulevard Mohammed V, my mother remarks that the street's monarchic namesake was fond of my grandmother.

"What do you mean? King Mohammed knew her?"

"Oh, yes. She was his manicurist in the 1930s. And she was very attractive, so he was naturally quite taken with her. He asked her to marry him."

"And she said no? To the king's proposal of marriage?" I exclaim.

"Well, would you want to live in a harem?" she replies. Fair enough.

After my grandmother's stint as the king's manicurist, she worked as a ticket seller at the old Cinéma Triomphe, one of numerous movie theaters in Casablanca. Hollywood had its golden age at the same time Casablanca did—they both were optimistic, hedonistic towns that turned on sea, sunshine, and cinema. In a place so entwined with its Hollywood incarnation, it is fitting that movie theaters should serve as landmarks. We decide to visit the best preserved and most striking example: the Cinéma Rialto, where Josephine Baker once sang her big hit, "J'ai Deux Amours." Recently repainted and renovated, the Rialto hints at a Casablanca comeback.

We curl onto a side street near the theater and stop for a mint tea at an outdoor café, where locals—some in jeans and Nikes, some in djellabas and the slipper-like shoes called babouches—sit on cane-back chairs under ceiling fans whirling with the languor of dissipating smoke rings, and tuck into chicken and lamb tagines and frosty local beer. In establishments such as these, my mother tells me, people used to lunch on grilled locusts—a delicacy during locust invasions—and Orangina.

By the café, I notice vendors ladling steaming bowlfuls of snails from massive cauldrons alongside bookstores selling folio editions of French classics. In these contrasts, I recognize my mother. Like her city, she is made up of Occident and Orient, of mismatched parts and various lives. I came to Casablanca to discover her haunts; I didn't expect to find her so vividly reflected in them. She is more like her Casablanca than I'd imagined. Maybe it's ancestral, but I, too, feel a visceral affinity to and intimacy with the country—its colours, its flavours (everything spiked with mint and coriander and orange water), even its pace, which tends to be at once lively and languid. In this, Morocco's Manhattan, locals rush to cafés—only to while away the afternoon there sipping tea.

On our last night in Casablanca we stumble into—of all the gin joints in all the world—Rick's Café. Housed in an old mansion and built into the walls of Casablanca's old medina neighbourhood, which overlooks the port, Rick's is a universe of Arab arches, tassel-fringed brass lamps, and potted palms. Dangling Moroccan lanterns spend their night sending shivering shadows onto white walls, while a bartender in a burgundy fez mixes cocktails behind a bar. Visiting European ambassadors sip champagne and dig into golden hillocks of couscous. Here, Rick is Kathy Kriger, who opened this saloon in 2004. (Like the movie Rick, she lives upstairs.)

"I wanted to bring the screen legend to life in Casablanca," she tells us. Kriger moved to the city in 1998 to serve as the commercial counsellor at the U.S. Consulate. "I fell in love with the architecture here," she says. "Then, a day after September 11, 2001, I decided to quit my government job and open Rick's. It was the gamble of a lifetime. I put everything I had into this place. I like to say that my budget exceeded that of the film's by about $50,000."

My mother and I order a pair of pastis aperitifs as a four-piece band begins to play Charles Trénet's 1940s tune "Que Reste-t-il de Nos Amours?" ("What Remains of Our Loves?"). The nostalgic chanson—about lost youth and young love—could serve as both Casablanca's anthem and the theme song to my mother's journey.

"Are you happy we finally came?" I ask her, risking hearing an honest answer.

"Yes," she replies. "Casa is more decrepit, sadder, but also more beautiful than I remember." She stops to listen to the snowy-haired saxophonist who, I later find out, accompanied Édith Piaf at her last concert at Paris's Olympia music hall.

It's almost midnight when we leave Rick's, knowing we're flying home early the next morning.

"I wish I could pack a little corner of Casa to bring back with me to Toronto," my mother says, already nostalgic for the city that knew her when life unspooled freshly ahead—at a moment when her life stretches largely behind her.

"Who needs luggage?" I reply. "You're already storing the sky and light in your eyes."

* * *

Olivia Stren is a freelance writer based in Toronto where she lives with her husband, son, and two cats. Her work has been published in ELLE (U.S), ELLE Canada, National Geographic Traveler, Globe and Mail, National Post, The Kit, Conde Nast Traveler's concierge. com *and* Marie-Claire Australia *among others. She's also been nominated for several Canadian National Magazine Awards in the Arts and Entertainment, Short Feature, Service Journalism and Profile categories. Some career (and life) highlights were getting to travel to, and write about: Barbados, Brazil, British Virgin Islands, California, Hong Kong, Finland, Kenya, Mexico City, Morocco, Spain, St. Lucia, Tahiti, Tanzania, Tunisia, among many other places. Among the people Olivia has interviewed: Michael Bublé, Matt Damon, Laurent de Brunhoff, Oscar de la Renta, Nora Ephron, Feist, Jane Fonda, Kate Hudson, Iman, Dame Daphne Sheldrick, Martin Short and Alice Waters.*

BITTERSWEET IN BANFF

Claudia Laroye

My father doesn't like chocolate.

Despite the fact that he married my mother, who is Swiss, and raised two chocolate-loving children, I don't recall my dad eating chocolate desserts, and certainly never an actual chocolate bar. As a candy-loving child, with the cavities to prove it, this suited me just fine. There was one less person to compete for the sweet stash of Toblerone, Cailler and Lindt that we would bring home from our summer holidays in Switzerland.

It isn't the taste or texture of chocolate that my dad finds distasteful. Nor is his disdain the consequence of paying for my expensive childhood dentist bills.

No, my father doesn't like chocolate because of the war.

Growing up, I didn't know much about my father's past. Like most young people who tend to think in self-centered ways that their parents could never have possibly ever been children themselves—inconceivable!—I too believed that my parents' existence began when I emerged into their lives.

For me, this conceit lasted into my teens. While I knew that my dad had been born in 1938 in northern Italy and had come to Canada sometime in the 1950s, the gaps in my knowledge of his early life were much larger than in the case of my mother's upbringing in Switzerland. She had reams of photo albums with dates and place names chronicling her family life, ski exploits and student year abroad in the segregated American south.

By contrast, my father had one solitary photograph. It was his Canadian immigration photo, a black and white image in which he was sharply dressed in his only suit, his blond hair Brylcreemed into the sleek style of the day. He was 19 years old.

The dawn of understanding about my father's childhood came on gradually, in flickering vignettes during my teens, in and out of focus like an old silent film. On my family's first visit to Padova, Italy, in 1982, we toured his hometown, which had changed greatly since my father's youth. After visiting the sites, including the impressive Il Santo, the Basilica of Saint Anthony of Padova, with its magnificent ceiling of azure blue and gold and the saintly remains of its namesake, we wandered in a residential neighbourhood, pausing in front of a series of brown, nondescript buildings.

What we'd come to see was no longer there. The orphanage, or *collegio*, where my father had lived after the age of 11, had been demolished many years prior to our arrival. In spite of its absence, my dad spoke to my younger brother and me with some fondness about growing up in the orphanage. He recalled how much he'd enjoyed going to school and studying math, his favourite subject, and playing soccer with the other kids. His manner didn't contain traces of bitterness; it was a simple and straight-forward acknowledgement of his adolescence.

It was a confusing visit. My father had parents; they were my grandparents, Nonna and Nonno. Nonna who cooked multi-course Italian meals with homemade pasta and five kinds of vegetables freshly picked from her backyard garden. And Nonno who loved to entertain my brother and me by pouring Labatt 50 ale into a glass to the point the foam would overflow onto their Formica table. Why had my father, who had parents, grown up in an orphanage?

The incomplete explanation that we were given was that times were different then. That answer fell far short of illuminating the past; like a stick stirred into a pond, the waters became opaque. Perhaps we were too young to understand. I filed that knowledge away as something I didn't really want to know.

When I graduated from high school in the late spring of 1987, my father proposed a dad-and-daughter trip to Banff, Alberta. I thought a trip was the perfect way to celebrate this achievement before I headed off to university. As I was the first of my family to be going to college, it was a source of some small family pride. I was excited about school and about our trip to Canada's first National Park, a place I'd never been. While we had taken many trips as a family of four over the years, this was our first holiday together, just the two of us.

Banff is beautiful at any time of year, and this late summer was no exception. The lively mountain town was buzzing with families and tourists from around the world squeezing every last ounce out of their holidays. We wandered along Banff Avenue and checked off our own activity list with a ride up the Banff Gondola and walks along the Bow River.

Alpine summers are brief and fleeting, and in late August, Banff's was preparing its exit. We wanted to make the most of our extended long weekend visit and headed west in our rental car towards Johnston Canyon, a forty-minute drive from town.

It was a beautiful day for a hike, and the seasonal change was noticeable in the air and in the surrounding forest. We brushed aside young deciduous tree branches whose leaves were already turning red and gold with the onset of cooler mountain temperatures. My dad was a brisk walker and set a steady pace. As we followed the trail through thc canyon, wc could hear and feel the rush of the waterfall, as well as the rumbling of a long, cross-country CP Rail train rolling through the wide glacial valley of Banff National Park.

Memories are often triggered by sensory experiences. Sounds, smells and tastes can transport one back to time and spaces previously lived, loved or endured. I don't know whether my father's memory was triggered by the vibrations and distant roar of the train, or if he'd intended to use this trip to share insights into his early life. After all, I was 19 years old, on the cusp of adulthood, at least technically speaking. He must have thought I was ready and mature enough to appreciate and understand what he needed to tell me.

Whether by design, fate or prompted by outside forces, he began speaking as we walked together side by side on the trail. Like the creek water, my father's words flowed from him in a steady stream.

Quietly and steadily he spoke about his childhood experiences in a manner that struck me as more surprising than sorrowful. As if he couldn't believe that he'd decided that this would be the time and place he'd chosen to share his past with his daughter. I was just as surprised and listened closely to his words rising over the rush of the canyon.

My dad was born and grew up in northern Italy during World War II. He lived on his uncle Augosto's farm in Montemerlo, a small village outside of Padova, one of the oldest cities, with one of the most storied universities, in Italy. During his early childhood, he lived with six female cousins who treated him like a brother.

He was happy in his uncle's home. Living on a farm had its advantages during wartime, and when he wasn't in school studying his favourite subjects of math and history, my dad enjoyed helping his uncle on the land. As much as a young child could anyway. In spite of the shortages that often accompany war, my father and his family were lucky to enjoy the food grown on the farm, including pears and persimmons, as well as the occasional chicken and rabbit.

When he was old enough, my father performed the daily ritual of walking through the countryside to school with his cousins. One day, their usual journey was interrupted by the rumbling approach of a low-flying plane which began spraying the ground with machine gun fire. The group threw themselves off of the road, rolling into a ditch and staying as still as possible. The plane was so low, it almost hit the stone chimney of a nearby farmhouse but managed to right itself and bank away from them.

Air raids were not uncommon in the region, especially after Italy's capitulation in 1943. Padova and much of northern Italy became part of the Italian Social Republic (also known as the Republic of Salò), the puppet state of the German occupiers and remaining Italian Fascists. The city hosted the Ministry of Public Instruction of the new state, as well as a military command post, railway station and an airport. As such, it was a strategic area for the Allies to target.

From December 1943 to the end of the war, Padova was heavily bombed by Allied aircraft. The worst hit areas were the railway station and the northern district of Arcella. During one of these bombings, the Church of the Eremitani, with frescoes by Andrea Mantegna, was destroyed; this is considered by some art historians to be Italy's biggest wartime cultural loss. The Cathedral and the University also suffered damage. Some 2,000 inhabitants of Padova were killed in the raids.

Fortunately for my father, he and his cousins were not harmed by the plane that day, or in the raids conducted by the Allies for control of northern Italy, or in the final insurrection by the partisans to rid Padova of the Fascists and German troops still occupying the area.

When liberation came in April 1945, there was much joy and happiness. Alongside their neighbours and countrymen, my father and his uncle's family fêted the Allied troops who'd entered the city and ended the occupation of the region.

As was common when young Allied soldiers arrived in a newly liberated town or city, GIs handed out candy and treats to local children. In Montemerlo, American GIs went from house to house, giving war-ration Hershey chocolate bars to all the kids. The GI who visited my father's farmhouse handed out chocolate bars to all of his cousins. But when he saw my father with his light blond hair and blue eyes, his reaction was swift and damning.

'Tu tedesco, niente cioccolata per te.'

'You are German, no chocolate for you.'

Northern Italy has been at the confluence of civilizations for thousands of years. Between raiding Gauls and Germanic tribes to the shifting allegiances of city states and empires into the 20th century, the Veneto region has seen its share of tribes, clans and people of all kinds, including individuals with all manner of hair and eye colour, from the prototypical black to light blonde and even red hair.

The misconception and accusation issued by the American soldier must have wounded my father deeply. After so many years of war and then occupation, nobody wanted to be associated with Germans, least of all a seven-year-old child. What was a day of celebration became one of confusion and exclusion. Certain memories are imprinted on us at an early age. That bar of chocolate became the symbol of my father's humiliation.

Among the falling leaves and flowing glacial water, a family mystery had been revealed. As we continued along the trail, I lagged behind, turning over my father's recollections in my mind, processing the words that, out of nowhere, he had put out into the universe, though they were intended for my ears only. On this beautiful, warm late summer day in the Canadian Rocky Mountains, his stories had offered a glimpse into his past, and revealed chapters of his life that formed the man he became, long before I arrived on the scene.

It was difficult for me to think about my father being so rejected as a child. To imagine his pain and suffering at the hands of others. I gained an appreciation about his formative years which made me grateful for how he had never let the negativity of his early life experiences cloud the way he'd raised my brother and me. Our childhood was filled with stability, love, parental involvement and family adventures. We lacked for nothing. I felt profound gratitude and love for how my father had overcome hardship, and that he'd chosen to reveal his past to me. This trip marked the beginning of our adult relationship.

* * *

In 1949, my father moved from his uncle's farm to the orphanage in Padova because his mother couldn't take care of him. After the death of his biological father in the Spanish Civil War, my dad's mother had met and married another man. I suspect my grandfather, with whom my dad had a tumultuous relationship, likely didn't want a young child around the house.

My father emigrated to Canada in 1957 at the age of 19. He didn't want to come. His stepfather had arrived from Italy the year previously to work and sent for his wife and stepson to join him in Montreal. My dad had just graduated from technical school and was working in his first job in a tool and die factory in Padova. It was a good job and he enjoyed it, but he had no choice.

On March 30, 1957, he and his mother departed on the Vulcania, travelling from Venice to Naples and then finally to Lisbon before crossing the Atlantic. He was one of the tens of thousands of Italians leaving his homeland behind in a large wave of immigration from the country that lasted into the 1960s. The Venetian custom authorities were not happy to see him go. Italy didn't appreciate their able-bodied young people departing when the country was still in the midst of post-war reconstruction. The officials made it clear that his return would be unwelcome.

My father and grandmother arrived in Halifax, Nova Scotia on April 9, 1957, and were processed at the Canadian immigration facility, Pier 21. Now the Canadian Museum of Immigration at Pier 21, this National Historic Site and landmark is where one million immigrants passed through on their way into Canada between 1928 and 1971.

After being welcomed into the country, their journey mirrored one taken by millions of others arriving on Canada's shores since the 19th century. They boarded a 'cattle train' outfitted with hard, rough wooden benches. My father was confused about why he was there, and why he was fed corn on the train, which was very unusual because in Italy corn was usually fed to the pigs, not consumed by humans.

It was one of many adjustments to come in his new life that would eventually lead to a long and successful career in the aviation industry. He reunited with his stepfather in Montreal, where two weeks after his arrival, a late spring storm blanketed the city in 20 cm of snow. It was his first taste of the more than 60 winters he's experienced during his life in Canada so far.

And like chocolate, he doesn't really like winter very much either.

* * *

Claudia Laroye is is a freelance writer and editor living in Vancouver, British Columbia, with her family. She is the founder of claudiatravels. com and is a contributing editor for Twist Travel Magazine *and deputy editor for* Vacay Canada. *Specializing in adventure, family, sustainable and wellness travel, her writing has appeared in* the Globe and Mail, Toronto Star, AFAR, Lonely Planet, Air Canada's enRoute, Vancouver Sun, Canadian Traveller, Explore, Verge Magazine, Fodor's, *and* Saturday Evening Post Magazine. *She's been interviewed as a travel expert by the* New York Times, National Geographic, the Globe and Mail, CBC Radio and Television, *and* Breakfast Television Vancouver. *Her favourite family travel destinations include Hawaii, Italy, Jordan, Switzerland and British Columbia. Follow her on Instagram and Facebook @itsclaudiatravels, and on Twitter @ travelling_mom.*

TRAVELS WITH DORIS

Jessica Wynne Lockhart

We would go north, it was decided.

It's a warm July morning when we finish loading up the Pleasure-Way. A small recreational vehicle about the size of a cargo van, it has everything we'll need for two weeks on the road: a queen-sized bed, barbecue, and library books crammed into every spare storage space. The plan is to drive from my hometown in northeastern Alberta, Cold Lake, up towards Yellowknife, in the Northwest Territories.

My dad stands in the driveway, watching us. His nervousness is palpable. It's been years since he was left alone in the house for this long. Hands shaking, he asks me, for the third time, if I know how to use the navigation system. I nod, trying to ignore the telltale smell of his breath.

And then we're off, waving as we pull away.

Not even 20 minutes later, my mom starts fiddling with the GPS.

"How do you set this thing up?" she asks.

The question grates on me. She's lived in northern Alberta for 35 years. Like any good Prairie girl, she could tell you what cardinal direction she was facing even if she was blindfolded, drunk, and had just got off one of those teacup rides at the fair.

"Mom, this is northern Alberta," I retort. "There's only one road and it goes north."

I yank the cord out of the cigarette lighter. The system sputters, its light slowly fading away—and with it, the last bit of control my dad has does too.

I try to change the subject.

"I'm sorry I'm so quiet," I say. "Mark and I have ended things."
This gets her attention.

"So he's single then? Maybe you should set him up with Chloé?" she suggests, referring to one of my friends.

She's entirely unaware that she's missed the beat.

My knuckles whiten against the steering wheel.

She needs this, I remind myself. We need this.

We stop for the night in High Prairie, sleeping in a campground beside the highway. After dinner, I go out for a run, the heat of the day still heavy in the air. I fly alongside deep ditches filled with foxtails; past the car dealerships, their lots full of half-tonne trucks; and down the empty main street. The sun sits low in the sky, casting long shadows. I'm a child again, trying to outrun my darker self.

It's the first run of many. Over the next two weeks, it will become my nightly ritual; an act that serves three distinct purposes: First, to listen my own music. (Early on, I'm forced to veto Santana. I don't find Rob Thomas particularly smooth.) Second, to escape the mosquitos and black flies. This far north, they orbit around everything warm-blooded, settling on every inch of bare skin the moment you stop moving.

And lastly, the runs are an excuse to get away from my mother.

* * *

I was 18 when I first moved away from home, making the pilgrimage to the city over three hours away. By the time I was 20, I had put even more distance between my parents and I—3,394 kilometres to be exact—by transferring to university in Toronto. But even before I left Cold Lake, my mom and I were never what I'd describe as close.

She was a pragmatic parent. In stark contrast to the parenting norms that dictated the '90s, praise was not a given.

One day in fifth grade, I came home from school, worried that boys liked my best friend better than me. My mom, in response, explained that it was likely because Shannon was prettier than me.

Everything that I excelled at—from getting scholarships to being published in a national magazine at the age of 17—was unexceptional.

"Why should I get excited?" she said. "These are all things that I expect from you."

Brutal honesty, a hatred of organized sports, and an unwillingness to bolster her children's self-esteem: These were the key tenets of my mother's parenting philosophy.

So, when I announced that I was going to spend my summer vacation with my 61-year-old mother, driving thousands of kilometres into northern Canada, more than a few eyebrows were raised. But although the trip didn't have a specific destination, it wasn't without a purpose.

Earlier that year, my friend Andrew's mom had a sudden brain aneurysm. She survived, but her memories died.

"There's a lot of things that I always wanted to ask her, but now I'll never know," Andrew told me. "It makes me sad because how can we really understand our own history if we don't understand our parents'?"

Andrew's words stuck with me. I had started to realize that I had questions for my own mom. I knew so little of her life before I was born and there were things I didn't understand. For example, why did my mom, who was friendly and outgoing, not have many friends? Why didn't she get her degree in library science? Why did she wait until she'd been with my dad for nearly a decade to have kids? And, most importantly, did she even want to have us?

It's maybe this last question that weighs on me most. I'm 29, the same age she was when she had my older brother. A year ago, I ended a long-term relationship to a man everyone thought I was going to marry over this very issue (he wanted kids; I didn't) and now I'm in the process of reframing what it is that I want my life to look like.

But it's an uncomfortable conversation and one neither of us is ready for. Instead, in the Peace River lowlands, somewhere near the hamlet of Guy, we push in amongst the bristly canola flowers, pollen clinging to our clothes. The brilliant yellow expanse spreads out in front of us.

Ten thousand years ago, the glaciers retreated here, flattening and dotting the landscape with lakes.

Ten minutes ago, I posted my mom's first selfie to Instagram.

* * *

As we get closer to the 60th parallel, I keep waiting for a dramatic shift in the landscape. But it never comes. Canola fields give way to the familiar forests of tamarack and white spruce, not unlike those found just north of Cold Lake.

I want to feel something foreign, something that will make me forget myself. The only thing that changes is that the bugs are now thick enough to form Rorschach patterns on the windshield.

I've long mythologized the north, an obsession fuelled by the relics from when my dad worked in the Northwest Territories. In our family room, a seal pelt was draped over the back of the couch (I'd tell friends that it was a cowhide; seals were much too cute to die) and tufted fur owls sat on the mantle. In my parents' bedroom, Inuit carvings of seal hunts hung on the walls. The furnace room was filled with rickety metal bookshelves housing dozens of dog-eared Agatha Christie novels—my dad's reading material of choice when he lived up north.

Dinnertime was punctuated by my father typing out Morse code on the kitchen table; a tic brought on by the desire to impress his know-it-all children. It was important, he insisted, that we should know SOS, in the same way that it was important that we should know how to call mayday on a CB radio. These were useful skills, he determined.

This was the time before GPS. This was the time before he started drinking. This was the time before my mom became his caregiver.

We stop when we see our first herd of plains bison north of High Level, grazing in the ditch. I pull over, not bothering to signal; we haven't passed another vehicle in hours.

"It's like they're posing just for us," mom says, excited and laughing. Her capacity to laugh and smile even in the worst of circumstances is one of her best qualities.

Yet, still stinging from my most recent relationship failure, I'm like a sullen teenager beside her. I pull further in towards myself while my mom happily chatters away.

Then, we're on the open sea. The pink-hued road rolls with frost heaves, skirting around the edge of Great Slave Lake and guiding us into Yellowknife. Mom puts on Neil Young's *Harvest Moon*, singing along off-key.

She was an unknown legend in her time …

Beside her, I'm quiet. I don't know what I was expecting. A movie-worthy montage of mother-daughter scenes? A non-stop stream of deep and meaningful conversations? Why did I think that two weeks in a vehicle would change the dynamics of our relationship?

And really, it was a perfectly good relationship. We both enjoy animals and obscure historical facts and music and long road trips and even each other's company. Why couldn't that be enough?

It's a relief when we finally get to Yellowknife. After days of just each other, we're suddenly surrounded. At Folk on the Rocks, Yellowknife's annual music festival, I pay for our tickets and we find a spot on the lawn. But instead of watching the stage, my eyes wander to the young families playing with their children, years before the teenage disdain sets in and years before brain aneurysms are capable of wiping the slate clean, erasing history.

Beside me, my mom lays back in the grass and smiles. She closes her eyes and 30 years slip away.

Once, when I was a teenager, she asked me if we were friends. For her, it was a rare moment of vulnerability, a rare moment where she was seeking affirmation for her parenting skills.

I knew exactly what she needed, but I responded with the same brutal honesty that I had learned from her: "You're not my friend. You're my mom."

She didn't bat an eye.

I had meant it as a compliment.

* * *

We spend two days exploring Wood Buffalo National Park. At the salt plains, I take off my shoes. The remnant of a sea from 390 million years ago, Grosbeak Lake is littered with smooth boulders and bear prints. Clay encrusted with crystallized salt pushes up, oozing warm between my toes. Afterwards, we drive to Pine Lake, where bison tracks cover the beach. I swat away horseflies and dive deep into the aquamarine blue. On the horizon, forest fires burn.

On our last morning in Fort Smith, we drive to Rapids of the Drowned. We climb down on the rocks, coffees in hand. My mom sits watching pelicans dive for their morning breakfast, and I sit watching her.

I think of the time my mom took my brother and I to see Joni Mitchell at the Edmonton Folk Festival. I was only nine, but she let me go dance at the front of the stage amongst the barefoot hippies. I was wild and free, my tiny arms and legs flailing to the beat. But by the time the music ended, the sun was gone. I wandered the hillside, looking for her, lost in a crowd of people larger than the population of my hometown.

When she finally found me at the lost kids' tent, I had tears streaming down my face. But I don't think she was ever worried. She knew that I'd find my way to a safe place—and that she'd find me there.

As an adult, I travel alone. I've lived happily without electricity and running water. I'm not afraid of spiders or snakes and I'm reasonably (although not entirely) comfortable shitting in the woods. I am, by my own standards, fearless and self-reliant. I am these things because of my mom.

I may never get the answers to my questions. But what I did know was enough. I didn't need praise and affirmations; I needed someone's unwavering belief that I was capable of growing into the woman that I was meant to become. And that, I decided, was more than enough.

Finally, it's time to head south.

As we do, the skies darken and the rain starts to fall. And, just as suddenly, an outpouring of another kind begins. Somewhere between Hay River and Manning, my mom begins telling me the story of her life before me.

* * *

Originally from northern Alberta, **Jessica Wynne Lockhart** *is an award-winning freelance journalist who splits her time between Canada, Australia and New Zealand. Specializing in ethical and adventure travel, her writing has appeared in* Outside, The Globe & Mail, The Toronto Star, *and Air Canada's* enRoute. *She's the Contributing Editor of* Verge Magazine, *a publication devoted to "travel with purpose," and the author of the forthcoming* Frommer's New Zealand *guidebook. Follow her @WynneLockhart.*

THE STORY OF US

Alec Scott

This is us, sometime in the far-off 1970s, three boys in the back of a ramshackle station wagon, hurtling towards the storied island of Nantucket. My brothers one younger, one older, are big for their age, but I'm small, the runt of this particular litter. The story of this trip, as we told it growing up, was that everything that could go wrong did, and yet, somehow, we all pulled together.

Whatever came between us later, we'd always have Nantucket, that island best known for its role in off-colour limericks. The line is out of Casablanca, of course, with the lovers, Humphrey Bogart's Rick and Ingrid Bergman's Ilsa, saying they'd always have Paris. Families can also have their romantic periods, where there's a swoon, where the amount of affection moving about greatly outweighs the acrimony. Here was a place, this spare, windswept island off the coast of Massachusetts, where we were taken out of our respective routines, where we looked up and saw each other—and mainly liked what we saw.

I now live in Northern California, while my parents and two brothers live in Southern Ontario. In the thick of this lock-down, with the border between the two countries closed for all but essential travel, I've missed them all, in an almost visceral way. And so, I wrote out my memories of that trip, hoping to get together with them, at least in my imagination. But the meaning of such stories shifts over time—the stories which seemed such a romp once upon a time, had other, slightly deeper, things to say.

The story really begins with my mother, with Lynne—and it ends there, too. She is probably the reason we ended up going to Nantucket from our home in a lakeside suburb of Toronto.

The daughter of a Canadian father and an American mother, Mom grew up in a suburb of New York, and then studied at Wellesley, the famous women's college also in Massachusetts. Though she liked the rigour of her classes, she didn't feel a fit there, catching her robe on fire at her sorority's initiation, and cursing roundly, in a most unladylike way, while she rolled about on the floor. Midway through her undergrad, she decided to transfer to a university in her Dad's home country, McGill. There she fell hard for Montreal, for the music and poetry of Leonard Cohen, for a new-to-her discipline, philosophy. I picture her walking the mountain, talking big ideas with her friends, young people from all over the world drawn to what was then Canada's biggest city.

And she also fell hard for my father. This young man named Simon was one of those kids from abroad, having left straitened, post-war England for a country, he thought, with a brighter future. He was outdoorsy, an avid climber and hiker in his youth, so the call of Canada's vast wild also beckoned.

Though Mom and Dad both loved their student days in Montreal, the opportunities for Anglos were in Toronto, and so, after a speedy, low-key marriage, they moved there, with Mom working an entry-level corporate job to help put Dad through law-school. Once he'd graduated and landed a job at a small but growing firm, they moved house to a suburb of Toronto, and started a family, us.

This transition from city to suburb, from working to mothering wasn't easy for Mom. She was McGill's top philosophy graduate, and had dreams of an academic career, of being a lawyer, a blues singer, a mystery author, of doing something … major. When asked to describe her in a Mother's Day project at primary school, my older brother said simply, "My mother is … a person."

While doing the bulk of the child-rearing, she tried to remain … a person. She carried on studying, doing a master's in philosophy at the University of Toronto, studying Hegel under the distinguished professor Emil Fackenheim. At the same time, my Dad was putting in the long hours required of a young lawyer. One day, on her way into the city for her classes, she dropped my younger brother off at his primary school, waving him off. Unfortunately, the school was closed that day, or they were out on a field trip—whatever, somehow she'd missed the memo. He was found later wandering in a dry creek bed. All ended well, but tongues clacked, fingers wagged. At around that time, she decided to sacrifice her high career ambitions to the commonwealth, for the good of all of us. If she'd been born a decade later, she might have made a different choice, but we three boys and our father were the direct beneficiaries of hers.

This all was in the backdrop as we trundled along in our station wagon, a chrome representation of our beloved Labrador retriever on its prow, singing American standards, all of us looking like extras in a Wes Anderson movie. (When I saw the *Royal Tenenbaums*, I felt pretty sure the wardrobe person had ransacked our closet.) With no videos to stream on a pop-down screen in the back of the car, we played games. One, A to Zed, involved being the first to spot a word on a sign beginning with these letters. In another, Countries and Cities, you'd use the last letter of the place named by the person before you to start your contribution, with Amsterdam leading to Montreal leading to Luxembourg leading to Guyana. We had to find ways to entertain ourselves, to find the resources within ourselves and in each other's company, to make the time not just pass, but pass enjoyably.

Unfortunately, we didn't always succeed. The boredom of mile after mile after mile sometimes would get to us. Or one of us had beaten the other too solidly at Crazy Eights, and revenge needed to be taken. My older brother and I fought so much that we often had to be sequestered in different parts of the vehicle, him way in the back-back, among the suitcases, me in a part of the middle seat not easily reachable by him. If he did reach me, even just to touch my shoulder, I'd scream bloody murder. Such restful times for our parents.

For this trip, my Mom had convinced one of her great McGill friends and her family to join us. Where my Mom was tall and blonde, Joanie was a petite brunette, originally from Nova Scotia, one of the best literature students of her year at McGill. Both women were book-smart, but both also loved a good time. Joanie recently told me how they once tossed roses from the windows of their room in Royal Victoria dormitory down to particularly handsome men in a parade passing below. Where my Mom had given birth to three boys, Joanie and her husband, also a lawyer, had three daughters, girls who were roughly our ages.

And so why not vacation together? We brothers might blow a breeze into the lives of these sisters who had intense, somewhat overheated relationships with each other, while the sisters might, one hoped, sand off some of our rough edges. Anyway, from our parents' point of view, maybe we'd entertain each other some, give them a bit of a break.

We didn't have an easy transit to Nantucket. With no Yelp reviews to access, we relied on brand identities, eating at known quantities—Howard Johnson's often, with their electric orange sherbet that we loved—and staying the nights at chains. The Internet might have warned us off one of the motels we chose, because it had a history of ticks lurking in its beds. But it hadn't yet been invented. And my father picked these bloodsucking insects out of our hair, as again, I screamed.

There's a long ferry ride between the mainland and Nantucket, and something about that in-between time calmed us, and then the island emerged from a shroud of mist, like Avalon did in the Tales from King Arthur storybook I'd read. The sculptural landscape was almost devoid of trees, with the homes, these classic New England clapboard numbers, dotted around. The island had not yet become the it place it would later become, but still, it had a certain cachet. Although we'd grown up near a Great Lake—Ontario was just a few blocks from our house—the Atlantic was a different thing, we all could tell that at once. For one thing, the smell was rich, somehow clean and cleansing, the salt piquing our nostrils.

Our little cabins fronted on it, and, on one of our first days, my father helped put together my older brother's birthday present, a massive orange-and-yellow, wood-and-fabric box kite. The plan was, they would send it up to dance around in the strong Atlantic winds. Alas, it was like a decent tennis player deciding to make her debut at Wimbledon. Shortly after getting the kite aloft, the winds made short work of the cord. I can still see, in my mind's eye, my brother sitting sadly watching those strong winds carry his birthday present away. I felt his loss as if it were my own.

We weren't a maudlin family—there could be no lingering with that loss. We went into the cobblestoned main town for a treat, this New England seaside staple, saltwater taffy. Delicious! We then went to a museum celebrating the island's long-ago mainstay, whaling. Museums and children don't always mix as well as parents hope, but the sperm-whale skeleton hanging above us was impressive, as were the docents dressed in period costumes, reciting nautical dialogue out of Melville. They activated my imagination, though maybe not in the ways they'd hoped. What would it be like to run a museum?

A bookish, quiet kid, with thick-lensed, often-broken glasses, I decided I'd make my own museum on our cabin's porch, spending hours gathering shells and driftwood, rocks and other miscellanea there. My opposite number among the sisters was also bookish, but much cooler than me, on her way to becoming a beauty like her mother. She called me Encyclopedia Brown after the bespectacled boy sleuth, who starred in a series of books that were popular then. After a couple of days of beachcombing on my own, I proudly showed off my collection to the sisters, making much of the pièce de resistance, my turtle eggs, these little brown spheres, clustering together. Maybe a little turtle would crawl out of these during our stay. They burst out laughing, "Not likely. They're rabbit sh- dung."

Always sympathetic, Joanie quieted her girls down, but what could she do? The girls were right.

It's a cliché that parenting was relatively freewheeling then, and certainly, we were left to our own devices a lot, under the care of a sitter, while the parents enjoyed each others' company over lunches with proper, non-Howard Johnson's food, and, every evening, with mixed cocktails. When the sitter was playing a game with the older children, my younger brother and the youngest of the three sisters spent a lot of time experimenting with kissing—she liked it and he, decidedly, did not, at least not with her. (Years later, she told me, on the basis of those kisses, "I knew he was gay." And when I told him her observation, he responded, "It was assault what she did to me.")

That said, at the end of each day, doing our different things, we would come together for a simple meal, and after that, Joanie's lawyer husband, a gifted raconteur, would tell us the latest instalment of the adventures of a rakish cat. The cat was resourceful and funny, triumphing over adversity in creative ways. It was a kindness that I still sometimes think of, that this man should have foregone the company of his peers for an hour each night to entertain us, taking time out from what was for him a hard-earned break.

I'm not sure why my mother took off on her own one day, but I suspect she made a deal with my father to let her have that luxury of kid-free time, away from our squabbling. Or maybe there just was an errand to run, food to procure. Anyway, she drove off, and gave her eyes the treat of this island, her mind the pleasure of some uninterrupted jumping from one thought to the next—some mental saltwater taffy.

But this was a trip where little went according to plan. On this nearly tree-free island, she managed to run the car over or somehow onto a big stump, taking out much of the car's underside. After the jolting stop, she looked around her. She was in the middle of nowhere. There was a farmhouse in the distance. To get there, she walked across a field full of wildflowers, the sunlight beating down on it, and asked its resident, a local, if she might use the phone. She called us, my practical father taking the line. He peppered her with questions about what had happened, getting more and more exasperated at the vagueness of her responses. He asked her that most sensible question, "Well, where are you, Lynne?"

"Oh, Simon," she said, "I have no idea where I am, but it's so beautiful."

It maybe wouldn't become a story in most families, but it did in ours. There was something in her which was hers, which would remain hers, no matter how much of herself she'd give away.

After Nantucket, we went back to normal life. My Dad worked hard enough to make partner, while my Mom ran a school teaching new Canadians to speak English, and then, with some friends, started a toy and bookstore on our suburb's main street. It wasn't the life of the mind she'd originally wanted, but it was something—and she made a success of both ventures.

As for us kids, those three sisters and us three brothers, we would all grow up, and we'd face our own highs and lows—and we three boys would get to welcome a young sister into our midst a few years later. Both me and my younger brother would come out, right into the thick of the AIDS crisis—and that was often, as you'd expect, rocky. For a time, I felt profoundly alienated from my mother, that ebullient person of many interests I'd so admired and loved, and she from me. In this tough time, Joanie again came through for me. She assured my mother that one could live a perfectly good, full life as a gay man—hadn't she seated my mother next to a successful lawyer, a man who also happened to be gay at her last dinner party? For that reason and others, slowly, ever so slowly, things got better between my Mom and me. There was never any ill will on either side, quite the contrary.

Telling these stories to myself in this time, the border between me and much of my family, I expected the stories to lift me—and they did. But they also laid me low, a small dip in a period when so many are facing such large losses. We were a family that played together, but we didn't somehow stay together. Siloed into different parts of that station wagon, we've chosen, as adults, to keep some physical and psychological distance from each other. There is no tragedy in this—we have our separate lives, our own friends and families. And there are consequences to my choice to live here, for various reasons, so far away from my people.

The sisters, meanwhile, as adults, have had their own accomplishments and let-downs, as one does—life. We never became friends exactly, the whole crew of us kids, but we're still in each others' lives—on that trip, we became, in that hoary old communist phrase, fellow travellers, nearly cousins, just as their parents became nearly an uncle and aunt. When the kissing monster came to San Francisco recently, we went out for a nice dinner, and gossiped about our respective clans and the wider circle of people we grew up in. She'd named my much younger sister the godmother of her first daughter and then, more recently, introduced her to the man who has since become her partner. The pair of them, sheltering in place in Brooklyn, at this writing, are expecting twins.

To celebrate our recent wedding at San Francisco's City Hall, my longtime companion David and I had a party at a friend's apartment in New York for our friends and family there, and my opposite number of those sisters, a photographer and realtor of Brooklyn brownstones, came, with her boyfriend. She told him, in a voice that reminded me of her mother's, how she used to call me Encyclopedia Brown—and how she found my extraordinary childhood geekiness somehow endearing. Travel together opened us up to each other.

When I re-examined these old memories, I also realized how dreams move from generation to generation in families. Certain aspects of my mother's unfulfilled ones made their way into the lives of her sons, while my father's realization of some of his necessarily less ethereal goals also bled through. My younger brother earned the doctorate that was always just beyond my mother's reach. But he and his husband have a daughter and so they do that same balancing act, of their own desires with her needs.

I had a false start career-wise, following my father into the practice of law, until I realized, ultimately, that I, I want that dreamy thing my mother had in the meadow. Such moments are rare—Virginia Woolf called them Moments of Being—but they happen more often in a writing life, I suspect, than in one full of court dates.

Writing professionally—that was something else she'd wanted to do, but never quite got the chance. (There is a draft mystery novel in a drawer somewhere about a murder on law firm's ski retreat, *Downhill All the Way*, its working title.)

My older brother didn't become a lawyer, but it was he who really followed in the footsteps of the diligent family men who were with us in Nantucket—working, on Bay Street, in the financial markets, to support his family of four, but also taking time out, after work, to properly be with his wife and to play his part in helping to raise their four fine children. "When I think of Nantucket, I think of time spent on my own, doing my own thing. I didn't mind so much the loss of the kite," he says. We were there together, but having separate experiences.

The trip left me with a feeling that one might travel, if lucky, in a gallant way through life. On the trip to Nantucket, we got ticks, we lost my brother's kite, my museum's opening was a bust and our mother nearly totalled the car on one of the only remaining tree stumps on the island. As a family, we had really no idea then what we were doing, driving along in that beat-up station wagon, singing and squabbling, playing games and staring out the window at the miles passing. Maybe, when you get down to it, we still don't. And yet, wasn't it all, isn't it all, sometimes, so beautiful?

* * *

A Canadian living in California, **Alec Scott** *was once a lawyer, but thought better of it. After leaving the practice, he became an editor at* Saturday Night *magazine, an arts columnist at* Toronto Life *and a producer at the Canadian Broadcasting Corporation. A decade ago, he relocated from Toronto to the San Francisco-Bay Area for his husband David's work. He has written on disparate subjects for the* Guardian, Los Angeles Times, *the* Smithsonian Magazine *and* Sunset. *His Canadian magazine work—for* Toronto Life, en Route, *the* Walrus *and* Report on Business—*has been nominated for 13 National*

Magazine Awards, winning three. His travel stories have been awarded a North American Travel Journalists' Association gold (for a piece on Germany's car city) and a Eureka! for the piece on California (for one on San Francisco's rough, historic Tenderloin) and have been frequently anthologized. He studied literature at Dartmouth College and Trinity College (Dublin) and law at the University of Toronto.

VISITORS FROM THE CANADIAN BUSH LOVE DELAWARE, ENJOY SHOPS

Helen Gowans

"A vacationing Canadian family reluctantly left Delaware this past weekend and headed their well-packed station wagon back towards their home at Snow Lake, Manitoba, 605 road miles north of Winnipeg." Delaware Gazette August 25, 1954.

You never know what remains from a family trip, what fuses in memory. But seldom does a lengthy, innocuous road trip by a family of five receive media coverage normally given to visiting celebrities.

In the summer of 1954, my parents packed up our family car, a gray station wagon, to undertake a road trip south, across the border into the United States; a family trip that would curiously form the subject of a feature in the local press at our destination in Delaware, Ohio.

We rarely had family vacations. My father had a hardware store which was open six days a week. He did have one other person working for him, but Dad was in the store every day and usually did accounting in the evenings and a portion of each Sunday.

> *"Mr. and Mrs. James Gowans and their family ... made the long trip to visit briefly with Mr. and Mrs. Arthur Field. Mr. Gowans is the brother of Mrs. Field and the two had not seen each other for more than 20 years until last week's reunion."* Delaware Gazette

How this trip came to be I really don't know. My Aunt Edith had recently married and became Mrs. Arthur Field, settling in

Delaware, Ohio. Edith was a journalist, and I suspect that is why our visit became an item worthy of mention in the local newspaper.

Our trip south started with a 36-mile drive from our home in remote Snow Lake along a gravel road to Wekusko, Mile 81 on the Hudson Bay Railway, a northern line of Canadian National Railway.

Snow Lake was *"a gold-mining town of about 900 population which centers around the Howe Sound Exploration Company Mine (an American concern.)"* Delaware Gazette

This route ran from The Pas to Churchill, Manitoba. My mother usually referred to it as "the steel." Vehicles, passengers and cargo had to be loaded and shipped by rail to The Pas (Mile 0) where everything was unloaded, and a road trip could begin. People liked to say CNR stood for Certainly No Rush as arrivals and departures were seldom on schedule. In fact, I remember one Christmas where the train was over 24 hours late.

My brothers, Don (16), Bruce (14), and I had only been in the United States once before, a fact that seemed to astonish our relatives. I was ten but can still recall moments of this big trip.

We spent long days in the car with no radio, TV, phones or other devices other than books. Mum didn't drive so Dad was at the wheel the entire journey south and back again. I tended to get car sick, so I didn't attempt to read. As this was the era of being seen and not heard, we weren't encouraged to talk either.

To pass the time, my brothers and I started to count the number of railway cars that passed whenever we stopped at a level crossing. I became familiar with the different types of rail cars as they rattled along the rails in front of our parked station wagon: flatbeds, boxcars, hoppers, reefers, cattle cars, tank ore cars, engines with company logos, and the occasional caboose. Our count reached 100 with the longest train. There were no passenger cars, only freight.

When we travelled through the Dakota states, my older brother Don stated that we must be somewhere near the geographical center of North America. And sure enough, we were. We briefly stopped to admire the 15-foot stone-faced pyramidal cairn that proudly announced, "GEOGRAPHICAL CENTER OF NORTH AMERICA RUGBY, ND."

And then there were the Burma-Shave roadside advertisements. In the early days of highway travel, the shaving cream company became well-known for its successful approach to roadside advertising.

The signs consisted of six consecutive small signs posted along the edge of the highway spaced so as to be read by passing motorists. I remember the ones with white lettering on a red background. We loved these and all five of us read them out loud with special emphasis on the last sign, which advertised Burma-Shave. Sometimes we even tried to guess the rhyming word or phrase.

Don't take
a curve
at 60 per.
We hate to lose
a customer
Burma-Shave

Our fortune
Is your
Shaven face
It's our best
Advertising space
Burma-Shave

One Friday we had a three-hour wait in a hot car for the ferry to cross the Straits of Michilimackinac, now called the Straits of Mackinac, in Michigan.

It was a hot summer's day; we had no AC and hadn't anticipated the wait. We were all hot, hungry and as cranky as we were allowed to be. There were no shops available and leaving the line-up was not an option. We spotted a nun in a traditional pale blue habit with a basket walking between the stopped cars. The only nuns I had ever seen were Sisters of Charity at Flin Flon Hospital when I'd had to travel for surgery. Those nuns were either dressed in gowns of crisp white or black. It was strange to see this one in less severe colours.

It was a bit windy and I remember watching to see how she'd keep herself modest. She was selling snacks, which struck me as odd; a Bride of Christ engaged in commerce! As she approached our window, we learned to our dismay the only snack available was smoked fish. Of course, it was Friday.

In their first home further north in Manitoba on Reindeer Lake, Dad had been a trader of furs and fresh fish. Mom was pretty sick of fish, and wasn't thrilled with the smoked variety, nor the nun selling it. But we were very hungry, and so Dad bought the smoked fish and we ate it gratefully. I expect there are no nuns selling anything there now; a bridge across the Strait was completed and opened in 1957.

"Gowans had left Scotland as a lad in his teens to join the Hudson Bay Company." Delaware Gazette

Dad traded furs in several Northern Manitoba posts and later, fish, too, for markets in the northern United States for a private trader. Aunt Edith became a journalist in the UK and later in the United States. Mom and Dad had carved out a life for themselves in Northern Manitoba which didn't seem to include their extended families.

Travel to and from Snow Lake could be an arduous and lengthy journey and thus visitors were rare. In all my childhood I only remember two visits, one over night from an uncle (Dad's Indian Agent brother) and one aunt (his sister, Jessie) for a few days. I had never really had the opportunity to see my father exist as anything other than my father.

So, when we arrived at 80 Orchard Heights, Delaware, I was stunned to see him, a tall handsome man with an easy smile, leap out of the station wagon to greet a woman who was also tall and looked a bit like him. She was wearing a belted grey and red shirtwaist dress and moved to him with ease and grace.

I had never thought of Dad as a brother, only as a father and husband. And because he rarely spoke of his childhood, I hadn't imagined him as part of a family other than ours. When Edith spoke, she had the same remnants of a Scottish accent as my dad. Although I didn't know the term DNA at the time, I was witness to its effect.

The joy in his face as he sped toward her and wrapped his arms around her was a revelation for me. She too held the embrace with the same joy. I couldn't imagine feeling this way about meeting my brothers who either ignored me or dismissed me as a nuisance.

In the backyard at 80 Orchard Heights, Art and Aunt Edith showed us a wooden table that held sand and a collection of shells from Florida, where they'd spent their honeymoon four years earlier. This was so exotic; I'd never seen the ocean, never tasted saltwater or held real seashells. In my bathroom even now rests a conch shell which I was given from that table.

"The local shops gave them special delight and they shopped for hours each day buying large quantities of clothing and shoes as well as items scarce in their part of the world … The Gowans were delighted with the fresh fruits and vegetables and the availability of fresh milk." Delaware Gazette

The American life, though I hadn't experienced it, was known to me from magazines and newspapers. It wasn't exotic; it was as I imagined.

As it was reported in the Delaware Gazette, it was exciting to be invited to "the Thursday two-hour showing of cartoons at the Strand."

However, there had been an outbreak of head lice and children needed to have their hair covered at public gatherings. We had no hats and, since my aunt and uncle had no children, there were none available for us. The solution was to wrap our heads in dishtowels from our picnic basket. I was mortified, even at ten years of age. But it was wear it or stay home. So, off we went, heads appropriately covered.

> *"The family so enjoyed their visit to Delaware that they plan a return trip."* Delaware Gazette.

In rereading the yellowed article from the newspaper, discussing it with my brothers, and searching my own memories, I realize that our family trip made a strong impression on me. We thought of ourselves as living ordinary lives but to this journalist we were foreign creatures from a distant, strange land.

I saw aspects of my father and mother I'd never seen before. They became more than my parents; they became separate individuals.

I never again saw my dad as only mine; he was part of another family. I recognized a struggle within my mother as she balanced our need for sustenance with her personal dislike for fish and nuns in habits. My parents became complex human beings, which was an unsettling idea at the time.

Surviving wearing a dishtowel on my head in public hinted that maybe I could survive all sorts of humiliation; a valuable lesson to learn at a young age.

The conch shell that I received on that trip to Delaware, Ohio, still sits in my bathroom. I occasionally pick it up to admire its scaly outside and creamy inside and reflect on what was and is.

* * *

Helen Gowans grew up in a gold mining town in Northern Manitoba. She attended University of Manitoba to study physiotherapy. It was a perfect choice for her and she worked across Canada and internationally. Since retirement she has pursued writing poetry and has studied at SFU.

She loves living in Vancouver and thanks her adult children, friends and many writers, especially Rob Taylor for their support.

WHY I DIDN'T CRY ON THE ROCK

Carolyn Heller

Until I had wedged my feet onto a narrow ledge high atop Canada's Whistler Mountain, my cheek pressed against the rock face and my hands gripping the granite, I thought that this story would be a different one.

When my 22-year-old daughter convinced me to climb with her up Whistler's Via Ferrata, a fixed "iron way" climbing route designed to get novice climbers out on the rock, I thought that this story would be about how The Kid becomes The Parent. How my strong brave daughter would coax me up the mountain as I hung from a cable, my fear-frozen limbs as immovable as the rocky peaks. That she'd say, "You can do it, Mom. Don't cry. Just keep going."

But that's not how the story unfolded.

As a child, I wasn't a natural adventurer. Cautious, shy, and a bit of a dreamer, I was that kid who was always immersed in a book. On the playground, I'd balance on the teeter-totter with my friend Jenny, each of us reading the latest tale of Nancy Drew, Girl Detective. I was active enough, playing hide-and-seek with a pack of neighbourhood kids, ice skating in winter, and riding my bike around town from spring through fall. Yet the place I was most likely to go on my bicycle was the public library.

So, when my twin daughters were born, no one was more surprised than I. Not only because they were the first twins anyone could recall in generations of our families. But because somehow, I'd given birth to two adventure girls.

When Michaela first pulled herself up to walk, Talia began to shriek. Though Michaela acted nonchalant about her newfound mobility, her sister—who'd been born much smaller and was not yet as strong—seemingly couldn't bear the thought that her closest companion had some physical skill that she'd not acquired.

From those first wobbly steps, which within weeks Talia had also begun to take, the girls hurled themselves into every activity they could. Gymnastics, soccer, circus, dance. Kayaking. Swimming. Rock climbing. While they'd cuddle up for nightly bedtime stories, they thrived on jumping, tumbling, and scrambling.

Which is how I found myself with Michaela one overcast afternoon in July, riding to the top of the Whistler Gondola in British Columbia's Coast Mountains.

"Are you scared, Mom?" she asked.

"A little," I said, trying to control the shaking in my voice.

We met our guide, Josh, outside the gondola station, and he led us into a musty shed, climbing gear lining the rough wooden walls. We each signed a waiver acknowledging that the activity we were about to do could cause significant injury or death.

Josh handed us white plastic helmets and fitted us for harnesses that strapped around our hips and legs. Michaela tucked her dark ponytail into her helmet and pulled her harness right on, but the unfamiliar contraption befuddled me. I eventually managed to step into it as if it were a pair of see-through underpants made of buckles, loops, and rope.

Dangling from our waist belts were two loops of springy red rope with a heavy carabiner on each end. Josh told us that these thick silver clips were what would keep us safe as we climbed.

On the mountain, we'll climb along stretches of cable, he explained, each about six feet long. We'll attach both carabiners to the cable, and when we reach the bolt at the end of each cable section, we'll unclip one carabiner and attach it to the cable ahead. Then we'll do the same with the second carabiner.

He demonstrated. Clip, clip. Then unclip, clip, unclip, clip.

"You have to stay clipped in at all times," he said. "Never unclip both clips at the same time."

He didn't say "or you can fall to your death," but he didn't have to.

"Ready, Mom?" Michaela asked. I swallowed hard and nodded.

Wearing our bulky gear, Josh, Michaela, and I, along with Maya, a guide-in-training, started out hiking through the rocky terrain above the gondola station. Worried that I'd be the slowest person to make my way up the rock, I was relieved that there were no other climbers in our group.

In a few minutes, we were tromping through patches of slushy snow. Josh stopped us in front of a silver ladder that was lashed to a smooth rock. A ladder that went straight up. And up. And up.

I started pestering Josh with questions about where we were going, what we were going to do, how everything was going to work. He looked at me, then at Michaela, and said, "Why don't you climb right behind me? That way, I can help you along the way. Michaela can climb behind you, and Maya will go last."

He clipped both of his carabiners onto the cables that ran alongside the ladder and nimbly climbed to the top.

My turn. I clipped in—clip, clip—and started up slowly. As I reached the pin that anchored the two sections of cable, I stopped and thought through Josh's instructions. Unclip, clip, unclip, clip.

Josh said, "Good, you've got this," as I stood up on the wide ledge at the top of the ladder and caught my breath. Michaela and Maya clambered up quickly behind me.

We walked a short section along the cable, before the next climb. This time, there was no ladder, just rock, with iron steps anchored into the granite. I grabbed one step, then the next, focused entirely on my next move. Unclip, clip, unclip, clip.

I looked down to watch Michaela ascend a section of the rock behind me. She climbed steadily, focused, her muscled body balanced as she paused for an instant to consider her next move.

The next section was harder. Although there were iron rungs at the bottom, they were spaced farther apart, and we needed to find footholds and grips on the rock itself. At one point, I reached for a section of rock, but it was too far. I was stuck.

"Josh?" He was a couple of sections of cable higher up and leaned down toward me.

"I don't know what to do next."

He assessed the position of my hands and feet. "Try stepping up with your right foot. Wedge it under that rock," he said pointing.

My shoulders strained to support my weight as I lifted my foot and hooked my toe into a crack in the rock face.

"Concentrate on using your legs when you climb," Josh said. "Your legs are a lot stronger than your arms." I nodded, biceps burning.

And we kept climbing.

When we took a short break to look out across the ridge of mountaintops, still covered with snow, I thought about how, as Michaela and Talia grew, I tried to offer them my own kinds of adventures. Together, we explored restaurants around the city where we'd sample Chinese dumplings, Dominican-style fried plantains, or skewer after skewer of grilled meats in a Brazilian churrascaria. Once, we spent the night in a local hotel downtown, where we swam in the pool all afternoon and ate breakfast in bed the next morning. When they were ten, we crossed the country on a six-week mother-daughter road trip.

Yet I needed to learn that the activities I enjoyed weren't always what they wanted to do. That sometimes, I'd have to let them decide what adventures they wanted to pursue—and whether I could, or couldn't, be part of them.

High on Whistler Mountain, I was finally starting to find a rhythm, looking for my route up each section. Right foot up. Left foot up. Unclip, clip, unclip, clip. Right arm reach. Left arm reach. Unclip, clip, unclip, clip.

We came to a ledge, with the cable anchored across it horizontally. I mentally measured the ledge and saw that it was narrower than my hiking boots. Below this strip of rock, there was nothing but air.

I was momentarily immobilized, trying to envision how to scoot myself sideways across this rock shelf without losing my footing.

Josh interrupted my thoughts. "Here. Let me show you."

He clipped onto the horizontal cable and said, "You think that the way to stay safe is to press yourself onto the rock." As he stepped onto the ledge and flattened himself against the mountain, he swivelled his head toward us.

"But if you're leaning into the rock, you can't move. When you're trying to hang onto the rock, you can't move your feet."

He suddenly leaned his upper body out backwards away from the ledge, and I tried to muffle a gasp. "If you lean away from the rock—I know it seems like the opposite of what you'd think—but if you lean out, you can walk right across the ledge."

The red ropes held him as he tilted back into the air, and he waved his arms out into a T to show us that he was secure. Then he turned and stepped across the ledge, like a gymnast tiptoeing across a balance beam.

"Come on," Josh coaxed me. I unclip, clip, unclip, clip, so I had both my ropes attached to the horizontal cables. Instinctively, I squashed my face against the rock, and I realized he was right. I couldn't move at all.

Michaela was quiet behind me.

The rock was cold against my cheek, and my knees were wedged uncomfortably against the mountain. My hands were in a death grip on the cable.

"Lean back," Josh said. And he waited.

I tried not to think about the endless space behind me. I knew that if I stayed clipped in, the cables would hold me, but I also knew that I could still fall. I imagined myself dangling by my harness, smacking into the rock as I swung back and forth.

Then I thought about Michaela, waiting and watching. I was terrified, but I wanted to believe, really believe, that I'm an "Adventure Mom." The kind of mother who's willing to dive into new experiences, drive myself to try new things, and show my daughters that life, despite its quite literal ups and downs, is one big adventure. I want to be the mom who encourages my kids to face their fears, to keep going on those days when everything feels hard, to push themselves beyond what makes them comfortable.

I was definitely not comfortable suspended on this ledge. Yet hanging from the mountain, with my daughter clipped in behind me, I found that, while I was scared, I was just as inspired. Inspired to show her that I could do it. That we both could conquer whatever fears we had, whether it's phoning a stranger or climbing a cliff on a 7,000-foot mountain.

I looked at Josh on the far side of the ledge, took a step, and leaned back. And suddenly, exactly as he'd said, I could move. Holding the cable lightly with my left hand, I pivoted slightly, and in a few seconds, I found that I had walked across.

I dug my toes under a section of rock and turned to watch Michaela, as she scampered along the ledge. "Good job, Mom," she said, as Josh snapped a photo of us. Later, when I look at the image, I'll see that we're both grinning.

As a parent, you're hard-wired to feel proud of your children, from the moment you hold their tiny bodies and applaud their first mewing cries. But there's nothing genetic that makes kids—particularly teens and young adults—feel proud of their parents.

I'm sure that someday The Kid will become The Parent and take away my car keys or tell me that I told her the same thing for the twentieth time. That's not the story today, though.

Today's story is that sometimes our kids will inspire us to do the things we thought we couldn't do. And when they tell us, "Good job, Mom. You did it," we'll feel just as pleased as when they got an A on their algebra test or scored the winning soccer goal.

The rest of our climb seemed to pass in an instant, as we reached the summit, unclipped from the last stretch of cable, and posed for more photos together. When we started our hike back down toward the gondola station, my daughter asked, "So, Mom, was it fun?"

"It was, mostly," I said, examining the lines of bruises that were already snaking around my elbow and marching across my knee. "And except for a few times, it wasn't nearly as scary as I expected."

I don't remember if I thanked her then, as we walked along the slushy trail, and she said, "Thanks, Mom. That was an amazing day."

But I'll thank her now—and her sister, too. For being my adventure buddies and sticking right behind me.

For pushing me to try something new.

And for letting me make my own way, out across the rock.

* * *

Based in Vancouver, British Columbia, travel and food writer **Carolyn B. Heller** *is the author of several Canada guidebooks, including* Moon Vancouver + Canadian Rockies Road Trip. *Her travel and food stories have appeared in publications ranging from* Lonely Planet, Atlas Obscura, Forbes Travel Guide, October Magazine, Canadian Traveller, Edible Vancouver Island, The Insatiable Traveler, *and* FamilyFun *to* Perceptive Travel *and* Roads & Kingdoms. *She has eaten her way through more than 50 countries on six continents, but she was unreasonably proud when her twin daughters once ate pig ears.*

CATHEDRALS, CACOPHONIES AND AN AQUEDUCT

Yvonne Blomer

Even with my headlamp on, I can barely see in front of me. I run my hand along the rail to mark where I am in this dark, dank tunnel that smells of mushrooms and muddy water. I can hear voices, of the people walking ahead of me, and the people ahead in their rumbling canal boat. I can also hear my dad and husband behind, waiting for a signal from me that no boat is heading into the tunnel toward us.

I turn and walk back, my dad sees me and puts his arm out to help me onto the boat as it heads into the tunnel, "Yup, all clear. There's a boat ahead of us going the same direction."

We are in the Chirk Tunnel, the longest tunnel of our trip, and I'd gone in on foot to make sure the passage was clear. After Chirk Tunnel the canal opens to a narrow, treed canal bordered by houses, grazing sheep and cows. Colwyn, my twelve-year-old son, is inside the longboat on the double bed listening to music on his iPad.

"Ah, here's Whitehouse Tunnel," I yell, now in the bow of the boat, my armpits tingling with anticipation. We know no one is coming toward us, as this tunnel is short enough to let light in from both sides.

"I'm heading in," my husband hollers so I can hear him from the bow.

"Yup," I turn and shout back, throwing him a "let's go" sign to make sure he knows it's clear.

As we emerge on the other side, I can see the rolling Welsh hillside to the left. I gulp. We've opened into a wide holding area just before boats are funnelled, when it's safe, into the Pontcysyllte Aqueduct.

The aqueduct is a two-hundred-year-old trough of shallow water, a mere three and a half metres wide and a whopping three hundred plus meters in length. It is the longest aqueduct in Great Britain and the highest in the world, at a dizzying thirty-eight metres above the rolling fields I can see as we enter, having waited our turn to cross this one-way cast-iron feat of UNESCO World Heritage Site engineering. None of these facts make it feel even remotely safe. My heart and stomach are in my throat, my husband and dad are thrilled and chuffed, my son and I are holed up in the cabin.

I walk past the two narrow beds in the ship's bow, and back to my son, mid-cabin, in the double bed. "Come on," I say. "Come and look, we are crossing the aqueduct."

From inside our long narrow canal boat, Colwyn and I look out the window at the trees, the fields, and the huge drop down to the valley below this narrow and rather old aqueduct. I prefer him to stay inside on this crossing, as there is literally nothing between our boat and the long drop down. Luckily, he likes the cabin and doesn't mind being inside. We move more slowly than the pedestrians who pause to look out at the vast valley and sloped hillside. The Pontcysyllte Aqueduct crosses the Dee Valley into the town of Wrexham in northeast England, near the Welsh border. Colwyn looks out, then looks at me, then looks out again releasing a long, low howl, like the little wolf he is.

We are on a family vacation in northeastern England. We started a week ago, flying on a sea plane from Nanaimo to Vancouver, then rushing to the Vancouver Airport so we could wait hours for our flight. After landing in Manchester and taking a transport van to the Roman walled city of Chester, we finally found our Airbnb, a converted church. Finding it was one thing, finding an entrance was another. We piled our rolling suitcases in the shade and took turns wandering around. I tried to get Wi-Fi to contact our hosts, but in the end, we asked another guest, and finally figured out how to get in. Relief enveloped us as we clomped up the stairs, my son nearly wilting into a heap, husband lugging hard cases, and dad ready for a pint.

We are four on this trip: my dad, who is in his late seventies, my son, Colwyn, 12, my husband, Rupert and me. Chester is on the Welsh border, near the town of Oswestry, where my dad grew up. We've started here because it is a fascinating Roman-aged city, and we are not far from Wrenbury Mill Marina, where we'll pick up our canal boat in a few days. Chester is not only convenient, it's also a gorgeous old city where we can recover from jetlag and explore without a car.

Our Airbnb is kind of astonishing. The upgrades and renos to create a cluster of small flats inside a once abandoned church have led to having the tall colourful stained-glass windows split by the floors between flats. So, we have a low window in our suite letting in colourful light, which is high on the wall in the suite below. The flat has two bedrooms, a cozy living room and a small modern kitchen. A coffee maker and packaged cookies are here, and Colwyn wants one right away. We make tea and coffee and catch our breath. I note beer and a bottle of wine are in the fridge for us, but we'll have to find the Tesco to add proper food later.

Chester is baking hot. Once we've had our snack, we all collapse for a while, with plans to go out for dinner later, find groceries, explore. Dad worries there are only two rooms and beds, but Rupert and I have decided and quickly convince him of the plan. Dad gets a room, despite his protests, my son and husband take the other room, and the shortest adult, me, takes the couch. Our sleeping arrangements are always a bit strange, I admit, it's part of the package when you have a kid with special needs.

Colwyn is twelve but seems younger due to physical and developmental delays due to Prader-Willi Syndrome, the rare genetic disorder he was born with. He also has Autism Spectrum Disorder. He is an awesome, fun-loving kid. Though born with low muscle tone and failure to thrive, he has worked hard to catch up physically. He can walk and jump and keep up on our busy days. Though, in this heat, he very much wants to sit or lie down and melt into a grassy lawn, or a bench.

One of the main defining characteristics of PWS is hunger; people who have it don't feel satiated. To help Colwyn not crave food all the time, we have him on a firm food schedule that includes breakfast, snack, lunch, snack, dinner. Even though we are travelling, we try our best to stick to the schedule. Even though the time has changed, and he may be hungry at odd times for a few days, we quickly set our clocks to Chester time. Sticking to a schedule, having a clear plan for the day, helps Colwyn cope with all the new routines, and allows for some predictability as we navigate new places and spaces. One way he's come up with to cope is to number the events of the day, from number one, morning coffee and books in bed, all the way to number 20, shower and bed at the end of the day.

On this holiday, Colwyn has also taken charge of what he'd like to do by focusing on one small passion. And that is park swings. Most days, no matter what else we are exploring, we are also on a quest to find a swing. Walking the walled city, all of us keep our eyes out for swings or playgrounds in the distance. Fitting in other sightseeing around Google Maps' predictions of the next park.

"Ah, look, I see one!" I exclaim as we walk the high walls of Chester the next day. We've stopped in the shade to watch a falconer work with his bird in a large field. We've tried a few of the locked doors along the walls, Colwyn knocking to see if a knight or guard will come out. We've marvelled at school groups learning sword fighting, in the ancient Roman ruins. A gaggle of them with their foam swords (pool noodles) fighting their teachers. School's not out yet in England. With the swing in sight, we exit the wall and navigate the streets. My dad is super healthy and fit, but has a bad knee, so sometimes he lets us head off on our wild goose chases for swings without him.

Already on our second day, after we drop down from the wall again, we note it is snack time and find a small café, with outside seating in the back.

Dad finally has his first pour and says, "I've never waited a whole day for the first pint when I've come back!"

Clearly our priorities are askew. The long-awaited pint goes down smooth and he and Rupert beam with their tall cold ales while Colwyn munches a cookie. We've quickly come to learn with the heat, and jet lag, that despite our desire to explore, we also need to rest. We need to carry Colwyn's iPad and his little zipper bag of Mini Munsches (Robert Munsch books) so he can have sensory breaks. We need fruit and water on hand and to be willing to sprawl in the shade or a café and take a break. Not just for Colwyn, but his needs often rule.

While in the café, Colwyn starts to let out little yelps. He has his mini books, and reads one, puts it in the finished pile, looks at all of us around the table, and then gives a half-hearted little "Awooo." To which one or all of us say, "Colwyn. What's your next book," or something similar, to distract him out of becoming louder and louder. This is a new development; one we are half excited about and half afraid of. He's finding his voice, albeit with extraordinarily little volume control and a fair amount of mischief.

Before we left our homes in Canada, I bought tickets to go to the Chester Mystery Plays in the Chester Cathedral. These plays date back to the 15th century, but for many years were lost, and re-found in the 1950s. Now they are performed in Chester Cathedral every five years. The plays tell iconic biblical stories, and this year will incorporate strong messages about global warming and plastic pollution with Christ wading through piles and piles of plastic. We arrive in time to eat dinner in the Cathedral Restaurant and, after exploring the cathedral cloisters, make our way to our seats in the nave. Colwyn is a bit tired and wired. He's been quietly threatening screams all day, so we are all on edge. Still jet lagged, we took some time in the afternoon to rest and are now hopefully prepared for the plays.

We are led to narrow bleachers set up in the Decorated Gothic nave, 13th century archways of brick with 21st century metal bleachers for seating. Once settled, we read the program and chat, people watch, and keep Colwyn busy.

We are squished into the end of an aisle, in the middle of a set of clunky, metal bleachers. I wonder what we'll do if we need to quickly get out. Colwyn sits between my dad and me, with Rupert beside dad. I watch a large group of people with disabilities as they are led to seats near the front, on ground level, with easy access. The woman sitting ahead of Colwyn has an unusual back to her dress, which crosses and braids at the middle. His hand reaches out to play with the pattern in the material. I hold his hands. With bordering-wild excitement he looks around the huge space, while rapidly chewing on his "chewlery". I chat with him about what we are going to see and how important it is to keep quiet during the performance.

Sometimes reminding him of the rules or expectations helps, sometimes it puts an idea into his head. He's relatively nonverbal but is beginning to speak more and more. He is becoming easier to understand. Experimenting with his voice, he is become more vocal, louder. He uses signs sometimes to clarify and uses a speech program in his iPad. His dad and I are adept at understanding his subtle communications. He may understand what I'm saying to him, but he's also mischievous. So even though he knows what I'm saying, he might think it still fun to yell out. The play hasn't even started, and I'm on edge. I give him a mint to chew on as the lights dim. My dad catches my eye, my husband leans forward. Colwyn puts his head in my lap and promptly falls asleep. One of his coping methods. I stroke his head and breathe a sigh as I settle in and watch the performance.

Though I know the stories, not from a religious background but from an English literature one, it is fun to see biblical tales from Genesis enacted. It's engaging to see how 21st century concerns are folded in.

Colwyn fidgets. My husband with his six-foot-four frame, adjusts his knees. We'll need a crowbar to unwedge him. My dad listens with his eyes closed. Colwyn abruptly sits up. I wonder if there'll be an intermission, when he says, "Go."

"We can't go, shhh."

"Go," he says, in a whisper, mostly because he rarely voices his words. He signs "go" then "home".

"Ten more minutes," I say. Which perhaps is a lie, an underestimate of how long it will be until intermission. Surely Christ will need to go on the cross before we can stretch our legs.

While I watch the play, keeping hands on him, his little fingers find the woman's dress, he traces his hand around the pattern. She turns. "Sorry," I say. She just smiles and shakes her head, no worries. People are marvellous, I think to myself, her back being stroked by my son's small cool fingers. Did it seem clear to her that he was different? Is it his cherub face and blonde hair? She probably also overheard our conversation during the beginning, about our worries. He traces and traces the pattern of her straps. Then sits up straighter, fidgets and looks at me.

"Go."

"Not yet."

"Home," he signs.

"Soon," I say.

"Awooo," he says, pretty quietly.

My eyes begin to scan, my brain calculate. Would I be able to, in my skirt, climb the outside frame of these bleachers and help Colwyn down without disturbing the entire nave? I quietly look around for an escape.

"Do you need to pee?"

"No no no nono." His voice a little louder.

"Shhh, soon we can go," I whisper. His dad sits forward and catches my eye. My dad, his hands on each of his knee, watches the play, listens to us. He moves a hand to Colwyn's knee. A bit of warm pressure there.

I look again at the special needs group on the floor, some in wheelchairs, some with cognitive disabilities, some visually impaired.

I wonder if there was a box, when I bought the tickets, for those tickets. Why did we never think of these things in the moment?

We were often in this kind of situation. Like in the flight over. I'd not prebooked meals, so Colwyn suffered the torture of people around us being fed, food nearly passing under his nose, him pointing to the right, and to the left, and signing "eat". All I had were fish crackers, which I didn't want to give him, saving the calories for the dinner that would soon come. I had water, he sipped. We waited. I promised myself I'd be more organized and never do this again. We'd have our plan firmly in place, and here we were, wedged and stuck and he was for sure going to burst out of his seat and disrupt the entire theatre.

Christ is finally crucified, surrounded by plastic sheets, yogurt containers, and Coke bottles. It's time for intermission. We pull Rupert to his feet, dad's knee is stiff, Colwyn drags me behind him down the metal steps. We all grab all our things and follow the crowd out into the open air.

"Phew," I say, sagging. "I think Colwyn has had enough, but I'm happy to walk him home and you guys can stay and watch," I say to Rupert and dad. They both kind of shake their heads.

My dad laughs, "All I could do was keep trying to figure out how we could get out of there. I thought for sure he was going to decide he'd had enough."

We all nod. We are, honestly, a bit exhausted, and fascinating as the play is, my dad then adds, "Besides, I've seen this before."

This is a family joke. Anytime a movie came out that was too much like any other movie, my dad would say he wrote it or had seen it before. In this case, of course, we all know the stories that the Mystery Plays are showing. Well, except Colwyn. We linger for a bit, Colwyn half pulling me along, and then agree we are ready to go.

We decide to head behind the cathedral and up onto the wall for a walk, as it isn't late. We can wander toward our flat this way, and take in the evening, the fading light, the beauty of the city and the many ancient ruins scattered inside and outside the wall. Colwyn is so happy now, skipping ahead, waiting, skipping and waiting for us to catch up. Whenever there are stairs, he waits for a hand to take his and support him down, out of habit at this point more than need.

He stops and points back, into the dark and says "Sw—."

To which I say, "No, no, not time for a swing, time for bed."

Now, nearly a week into our vacation, we have opened and closed canal locks, watched the boat rise as the lock flooded, and sink as it drained. We've walked into villages to find food, to find the swings, eat ice cream, feed ducks. We've photographed hundreds of canal bridges, steered, or walked alongside the boat, sat in the bow, lay on the beds.

When we first arrived, after a complex and harrowing cab ride from Chester, our two-bathroom, one double, two singles, full kitchen boat seemed just heavenly. Our own space, utter bliss for Colwyn, and as a result, for the rest of us too. It's one of our must-haves when travelling with Colwyn, our own private space. Sometimes that means renting a car rather than taking public transport, as the car can be our own world. Sometimes it means skipping parts of a trip we'd planned—say to stay in Oxford longer rather than visit London because of the heat and the crowds.

Once settled into the boat, and on our slow way, we quickly decided the single beds were too narrow for Colwyn, so he and I shared the double and dad and Rupert became roomies at the bow of the boat. My dad nearly rolled out of his bed the first night, and Rupert couldn't stretch his legs out, so they switched. Eventually, Rupert moved to the foldout bed/ dining table which was even longer.

Our days are spent puttering along, pulling into grassy areas for lunch time picnics, walking alongside the boat, which frankly makes Colwyn nervous, even though it's easy to get back on. He dons his life jacket, which we brought with us, if he sits outside on deck during any complex manoeuvres. Often, he howls as the boat rises and falls in the lock systems. I tell him frequently that this water is not for swimming, not clean, not good water. We watch crows, eagles, cows, sheep, pass a Bed and Breakfast my mom and dad stayed at years ago, eat in a pub they'd been to on their last visit to England before she was too unwell to travel.

Rupert loves captaining the boat. I love opening and closing the locks. Dad revels in all of it. Colwyn loves the boat, the bed, unfettered down time, exercising his voice, slow walks alongside and daily quests for swings.

And here we are, the ultimate experience—crossing the Pontcysyllte Aqueduct. As we slowly cross the aqueduct, following the boat ahead, and being followed, Colwyn howls. Crossing is a slow process, slow as Ents moving over middle earth, or snails, slow as turtles. I point out the window, he stands behind the table and points where I'm pointing. I talk about what we were doing, that a village is on the other side, and we could also visit Llangollen. Us three adults have discussed back and forth if we'd take the canal to Llangollen, a full day there and back, or catch a bus to explore, a half hour bus ride. We haven't landed on a final decision, but dad is leaning toward a day of reading on the boat, and we are mulling a bus trip and possibly a village swing.

Colwyn looks out the window, and points at the vastness of green, the big drop, the perfectly engineered arches of the structure, he lets out another whopping howl. And this time, I join him.

"Awoooooooooo," we howl.

Dad peeks in.

"All good here," I say, giving a thumbs up. Colwyn breaks into a stream of giggles.

We amble our way across. It's true, you can easily step off the boat, onto the pedestrian part, which dad does to take photos. But our boat is open on both the right and left side, and a step off the left would land you a long way down.

We howl our slow way across. I keep my mental focus, my feet firmly planted inside the boat, do not let my mind wander to the sky, the drop, the massive arches, the thin, thin sides of the iron canal. Its age.

Once across, we quickly, with an awkward U-turn, find a spot to moor and tie up. Once we are settled, have had a beer and a wander, Rupert texts my nearby cousins, who drive down from Oswestry. Colwyn gets to meet new family members: Jamie, a grown-up cousin of his generation, and my dad's youngest sister's two daughters, Sue and Jackie, and Jackie's husband John. He is enthralled. He practices saying their names: Jamie, John, Jackie, Susan, over and over again. We take their photos and add them to his speech app in his iPad. We eat a delicious pub dinner. When bored, Colwyn rests his head on the table, and closes his eyes. We drink. He sits up, says everyone's name and howls.

I will come to accept, to a point, this howling in public spaces. Every time I'll say, "Now Colwyn, if you want this (usually music on his iPad) you need to stop that (usually howling)."

To which he'll say, "No, no, no," and then howl again. While John will say, every time, "Don't worry, nothing to worry about, we're all noisy." and Colwyn will catch his eye, giggle, and howl again. To which my dad will jostle Colwyn's leg, and my husband will lift his pint to his smiling lips.

* * *

Yvonne Blomer is an award-winning poet, and author of the critically acclaimed travel memoir Sugar Ride: Cycling from Hanoi to Kuala Lumpur. *Her most recent books of poetry include* As if a Raven *and the anthologies* Refugium: Poems for the Pacific *and* Sweet Water: Poems for the Watersheds, *which she edited for Caitlin Press. She is the past Poet Laureate of Victoria, B.C. and lives, works and raises her family on the traditional territories of the WSÁNEĆ (Saanich), Lkwungen (Songhees), Wyomilth (Esquimalt) peoples of the Coast Salish Nation.*

INTO THE WIND

Lynn Easton

I brace my paddle against the gunnels of this old canoe, take an awkward step inside with one tentative foot and fall flat on my face, flailing like a fish out of water.

My two teenage daughters guffaw, but I'm not laughing.

It's windy, it's cold, and I am petrified as I am about to embark on my first-ever family backcountry trip on the famous Bowron Lake canoe circuit in British Columbia's Cariboo country.

It's not that I can't canoe or that I detest the outdoors. I started to embrace the iconic Canadian pastime before these two were born, when their father and I first bought this faded green relic with wedding money meant for more practical things.

But we'd just moved to an idyllic rural Fraser Valley property on the banks of a wild slough. It was teeming with life: eagles, otters, ducks, beavers. We longed to reach further into their world.

So, we bought the canoe. I learned to J-stroke on this gentle serpentine slough. Learned to read the water for snags and slack tides, the sky for wind and worsening weather.

My daughter must have felt the waves in-vitro because she came out a paddler. She preferred to fall asleep to the sound of the slough. And used a plastic yellow shovel as a paddle until she graduated to her own tiny honey-coloured lacquered cedar beauty still stored somewhere in the depths of her teenage bedroom.

So, paddling is an important part of our family's outdoor fun. But still, I have never once gone on a single one of my crew's backcountry canoeing adventures.

I tried once. When my girls were preschoolers, they both got bear bells and binoculars and we headed to BC's Clearwater Lake for our first big backcountry trip. But a stern park ranger put an end to that plan when she closed down the park due to a fluke tornado, sending us back down the 71-kilometre dirt and potholed road. I refused to return the next day. The idea of risking my children's lives suddenly felt neglectfully frivolous and dangerous.

That fear ran deep, and I have never managed to shake the feeling.

For almost an entire decade, I've avoided all attempts to get me back into the wilderness. I have, however, managed to do the mental gymnastics needed to encourage my daughters' adventures with their dad and waved them all goodbye and into their yearly adventures. And I've made all the right noises when they returned with tales of gorgeous night skies and encounters with wildlife.

But still, I fretted from the time they left until they got home, a messed-up mix of panic and relief that I wasn't with them.

Yet, here I am now, falling into this boat in an inauspicious start to this four-day circuit of the west side of the Bowrons. My family has previously done this route but can't wait to show me this place where they feel most alive, most competent, most joyful.

The girls have chosen to paddle together and have pushed off ahead of us. After laughing at their mother's debut, they are itching to get moving.

"Slow down, slow down," I yell before they've have gone 100 metres.

I watch them bob up and down in the growing waves and want to leap from my boat and into theirs. I want to turn it around and take us all to some warm, cozy spot to watch this squall from shore.

But I am out of luck. With the wind up, and the girls ahead of us, I have no choice but to start paddling hard as we head across the 7-kilometre-long Bowron Lake, the biggest of the four lakes we will see on this trip.

We should cross within an hour, but this wind means it will take us at least two. I look to their boat with every stroke. They are drifting away from us but can still hear my calls.

"Slow down, slow down."

They do and the eldest steers toward us for no other reason than to keep me from freaking out.

As she does, the wind begins to settle a bit. I breathe into a rhythm, seeking assurance that they are ok. I try to see the beauty in their tandem movements. People mistake them for twins all the time. And it's my turn to marvel at their synergy.

We make it to the campsite. I'm exhausted and make an irrational deal with myself that I can declare this the end of the trip if we want. I can convince them not to go further and to explore the water and the woods from here. But even as I think this, I know that's not how the Bowron Lakes are meant to be explored. It's supposed to be a challenge. You are supposed to be uncomfortable. You are supposed to feel small and at the mercy of nature.

But I am still unsure why.

While I sit numb-limbed and blank-faced on a rock, they get to work. I can't move, useless in my fatigue and lack of experience. The backcountry camping stove is boiling water in minutes and someone hands me a hot chocolate. The tent is up next. I watch my girls in their whirlwind state as they tie knots on rain tarps, build fires, and pull canoes up a steep embank to prepare for sleep.

The four of us barely fit in the tent anymore. But we are happy for the close warmth as we fall asleep to the chirp of chipmunks, which I mistake for cougars, but am too tired to worry. At the crack of dawn, they start the routine in reverse. Tent taken down, breakfast made on the open fire, canoe packed full of food and clothing and we are off again. This continues for four days, just as planned. We haul the boats out and portage them through muddy trails on unwieldy wooden trailers in a confident routine of growing skill and strength.

I relax a little as the weather warms and the lakes get smaller. Maybe too, I see my daughters grow taller in front of me. Their paddling muscles taut, their confidence palpable.

My eldest is assigned to paddle with me for a while. She is a pro. After her years on the slough she began solo racing at nine years old and became a bona fide champ by the age of 12.

But it's not the racing she loves, I discover. She wants to take it easy, explore the shorelines, slice silently through water to identify mosses and hope for a glimpse of moose. My heart slows down with her in the boat. I give in to her expertise.

And one hot, breathless afternoon on the third day, I am actually joyful.

My eyes are closed. I feel the lull of the rocking canoe as her constant, steady strokes move us forward. Her sister starts singing. She and her sister sing a lot, but I haven't heard it bounce off the granite of a rock face before. I push away the thought of what I have missed in the past decade and listen. We don't talk about the fact our trip is almost over. Or that we will get up in the morning and head back over the long lake we started on. I realize though, that the water wasn't nearly as treacherous as I'd imagined that day.

I don't admit this to any of them and hop in the boat the next morning with a deep breath, thankful for the calm water. But within a half hour that unpredictable breeze turns into a real storm with waves hitting us sideways and threatening to knock us straight out of the boats. We paddle hard but stay in place.

I have to scream to be heard by Jesse. She looks concerned as she tries to give me instructions to reach deep into the water with my paddle to help her move the boat. But as the front of the boat dips sharply up and down over the cresting waves something odd comes over me. I start laughing.

"Woohoo, I can't reach the water," I yell back at her. "I can't reach it."

In this wild water, it feels as if we are voyageurs speeding through the rapids of the Fraser River and I have complete confidence in my captain. Strangely, to all of us, I have no fear. Not for me. And not for my children.

My partner has manoeuvred his boat to head into the waves, a trick to keep from capsizing. I feel Jesse fight to follow suit. I know I'm little help to her with my lame attempts to paddle in this wind. I should be more concerned than I am. But I have seen her fight these kinds of waves in competition. I have seen her show me her prowess on this trip. I know she will be ok. We will be ok.

It feels like a letting go and a return as I ride these cresting waves. I remember feeling her heartbeat as a newborn in our shiny new canoe floating down the slough. How can I keep you safe? I thought. How do we navigate this journey together? I still don't know the answer. But I guess I know now, finally, that there is something to be said for the unknown, the unpredictable, even the dangerous. Something on the other side worth leaping into a boat for.

Jesse is frustrated with my laughter. She is working hard to get us home and needs some help, so I hunker down and paddle hard. I am still smiling to myself as we count off our strokes and gain a strong, unstoppable rhythm that is part hers, part mine. Together, we head for the shore.

* * *

Lynn Easton writes from her home on Katzie territory in Maple Ridge, British Columbia. Her creative non-fiction and poetry appear in Boobs *(Caitlin Press),* Sustenance *(Anvil Press) and in The Malahat Review where she was the 2016 winner of The Constance Rooke CNF Prize. She also writes community newspaper columns about family and early child development.*

ON THE TRAIL TO CIVIL RIGHTS

Heather Greenwood Davis

On a trip to Alabama, I showed my teen son the history of the civil rights movement.

Most of the monologues that I deliver at my house start out as an attempt at conversation with my teens. I raise some issue in the news, mention a similar event from the past and within a few minutes, their glazed eyes tell me they've moved on to counting down the moments until they can return to their game of Fortnite.

It's frustrating, but I get it.

I remember my own parents trapping me as I tried to tiptoe past them while they watched the evening news. Despite their insistence, I paid little attention to the major events of the day.

This, despite being only a few years removed from the American Civil Rights movement of the sixties, being alive during Muhammad Ali's Rumble in the Jungle and being well into my teens when Nelson Mandela was released from prison.

Huge historical events were happening right before my eyes, but they felt as foreign to my life as the First World War lectures in my classroom.

Recent news events that have women's marches, Black Lives Matter protests and political warfare as front-page news, feel like history revisited. But for my kids, despite the fact that these events will have a direct bearing on what they learn, how they're treated and who they become, it's the equivalent of being trapped to watch the evening news.

Add social-media streams that make it possible for them to avoid any news that feels un-fun, and you have a generation of teens who may be even more removed from historical lessons than I was.

If I was going to get their attention, I'd need to shake things up. So, in June 2018, I took Cameron, my 13-year-old son, to Alabama.

Maybe, if he stepped into the places where civil-rights history was made, he'd have a greater sense of its importance. My timing couldn't have been better. The US Civil Rights Trail was launched in 2018 and highlights more than 100 sites across 15 states that were pivotal to the movement. In Alabama alone, there are at least 28 such sites.

We start our tour in Birmingham. The corner of 16th Street and 6th Avenue North where we meet our tour guide, historian Barry McNealy, is central to any civil-rights discussion. Behind us is the Civil Rights Institute—part museum, part gallery and part historical archive. But the church across from us is what drew me here.

On Sept. 15, 1963, in Birmingham, the 16th Street Baptist Church was bombed by the Ku Klux Klan. Inside, four schoolgirls—Addie Mae Collins, Cynthia Wesley, Carole Robertson and Denise McNair—were killed as they prepared for Sunday school.

Three of the girls were 14 years old. The other was 11.

As McNealy tours us through the church and tells the story of the girls, I watch it register with my son. The historical events that involved kids his own age made the stories relevant for my son. But then McNealy says something I hadn't heard before: The girls weren't the only ones in the church that day.

Upstairs, Carolyn Maull, a 14-year-old Sunday school secretary, was in the church office. When the phone rang that morning with a warning of a bomb blast in three minutes, it was she who answered. And when it exploded, blowing her off her feet and killing the girls below, she survived.

McNealy continues the tour by leading us across the street to the monument for the girls in Kelly Ingram Park.

There, we stop to hear how Martin Luther King, Jr. arrived after the blast, rallied the children of Birmingham and set them out on what would become known as the Children's Crusade. Children, by some reports as young as six, would leave the church, 50 at a time, with an intention to protest segregated lunch counters, shops and buildings. Most didn't get farther than this park, met by armed tanks, high-pressure firehoses and dogs sent by the Birmingham police.

Standing in the spot where it happened sends chills across my skin. There were children the same age as my son who were knocked to the ground in this park. There were parents just like me who had to watch it happen.

At the time, the news accounts of this march would lead to an international uproar and become a pivotal moment in the movement. As we listen to McNealy, a woman passing the group stops and says hello. McNealy introduces her as "Ms. Carolyn McKinstry." She offers quick pleasantries and continues across the street.

McNealy seems surprised we aren't more interested. He points at the church and repeats her first name as she leaves. The possibility hits Cameron and me at the same moment: This Carolyn is that Carolyn. Carolyn Maull is now Carolyn McKinstry. We say it out loud and McNealy nods in excitement. It was as if Rosa Parks had stepped off the local bus, said "Hello, I'm Rosa," and then continued on to Costco.

I'm rendered speechless but Cameron springs into action. He takes off running and catches up to her down the street. From my frozen spot in the park, I watch them chat, hug and—as is required of any teen traveller—attempt to take a selfie. When that proves too tough, they stop a passer-by (who we'd later find out is Andrea Taylor, the director and CEO of the Civil Rights Institute) to help. He returns to me beaming.

"That was her!" he says to me shaking his head in disbelief. "That was her."

There isn't a story we hear on the rest of our trip through Alabama that isn't affected by that moment. This history isn't age-old. It's alive and breathing and waiting for us to meet it. My monologues have had a little more weight ever since.

* * *

Heather Greenwood Davis is a Contributing Writer and on-air storyteller for National Geographic *and a freelance feature writer with* The Globe and Mail. *She has been reporting and writing stories professionally for more than 20 years. A recognized expert in the industry, her work appears in popular print and digital publications, most recently* Afar, Travel and Leisure, EnRoute, Outside *and* Virtuoso Life. *She is also a trusted expert on television (including* Good Morning America, The Social on CTV, CHCH *and* Global Morning Live*). Her travels and experiences have also been featured in* O Magazine *and on* NPR. *Heather was named the Family Travel Association Person of the Year in 2020 and a National Geographic Traveler of the Year in 2012. Though her work encompasses far more than traditional family travel stories, she is also the voice behind GlobetrottingMama.com—an international travel, family focused blog that features the adventures she takes with (and without) her husband Ish and their two sons, Ethan and Cameron. Heather's work can be seen at www.heathergreenwooddavis.com. She lives in Toronto, Canada. Facebook: GlobetrottingMama Twitter & Instagram: @ByHeatherGD*

SUMMER IN THE TIME OF COVID

Jennifer Bain

I think of Air Canada most when I'm driving. Like this summer in northern Ontario, taking the scenic route home from the cottage to Toronto along Highway 64 from Verner to the French River. It's nothing but family farms, small towns, quiet rivers, empty lakes and pine forests here, at least before making a sharp left south on Highway 69 and winding through the western edge of Muskoka. The July sun was shining. The two-lane highway was mostly empty. The minivan gave the four of us much-needed personal space to relax and stare at the world while we blasted classic rock and outlaw country. We had nowhere to be except in the moment.

From the back seat, Charlie gave a tell-tale whimper. He's 7, a picky eater, rake thin and the only fair-haired child in a family of brunettes. Whatever sunshine lightly tanned his ghostly face during this week at Bain Lake   the speck of a lake named for his great-grandfather—has abruptly disappeared.

I knew that look. "Get the bag," I said calmly. Charlie reached for the Air Canada motion sickness bag tucked under his booster seat, bowed in defeat over it and started loudly retching. I pulled over on the narrow shoulder, jumped out, whipped open his door and stood by patiently waiting for the heaving to stop while muttering soothing words.

Airline barf bags are a miraculous thing. Bigger than needed. Sturdy. Air Canada's bags have wire tie closures so they don't leak before you find a garbage can. People collect these precious bags and sell them as "vintage" on eBay. I'm not ashamed to admit I grab a few every time I fly, which until the pandemic hit in

March 2020 was at least 50 flights a year. Of all the airlines I've experienced, Air Canada makes the best barf bags.

My son doesn't barf every time we hit the road—just randomly enough to keep me on edge. Vomit or no vomit, though, travelling is wasted on my children.

Maybe we are Sauble Beach people.

The impulsive idea came to me four months into the pandemic when we had all gone mad from togetherness and after reading about the millennials who transformed a retro motel in Picton and were now taking their pink colour schemes and love of rosé to Sauble Beach. They called it "the retro beach town that captured our hearts in just one visit," and showed off enticing photos of the iconic "Welcome to Sauble Beach" sign. The young moteliers talked of yoga on the beach, a groovy taco bus and healthy smoothie bowls, and it all sounded like an antidote to quarantine.

The only catch was that the 24-room motor lodge with a pool and dining lounge wouldn't be ready to open until September. Instead, I googled Sauble and randomly nabbed a late August week at a no-frills, two-bedroom cottage and paid in full in advance. Rental cottages were in high demand this summer, and I was pleased with myself for scoring one for my family. We would have to bring our own linens, pillows and food on top of the usual luggage. We would be required to clean up and leave it as we found it or forfeit the $300 damage deposit. Still, I looked forward to the trip.

My Ontario summers have always happened in cottage country north of Toronto, first at my family cottage when I was a kid, then at summer camps (a different one each year because I've always hated doing the same thing twice), and then back at my family cottage when I was a single mom and money was tight.

Beach towns sounded novel, and Sauble isn't far from the Grotto, a much-photographed cave with a pool of gorgeous blue water in Bruce Peninsula National Park near Tobermory. I successfully navigated the Parks Canada reservation system and nabbed a four-hour parking time slot and four admissions to hike to the Grotto.

"I'm not going," was Charlie's matter-of-fact response to the news of the Sauble trip.

"I'd rather stay home," his tween sister Hazel snarled. "Do I have to go?"

How did a travel writer wind up with two defiant homebodies? The same way, I suppose, that I wound up with a defiant eight-year-old vegetarian when I was a food writer and dragged by oldest daughter Lucy on near constant culinary adventures.

I try not to envy my colleagues who seem to be successfully nurturing eager young travellers. I secretly wonder if their kids would also, if given the choice, rather stay home.

We squabbled most of the drive up to Sauble, about whether the kids had to go to the Grotto (yes, since they're too young to stay alone), about whether they would have to leave the cottage (no, we would take turns staying inside with them), and about why we detoured to see the Wiarton Willie statue. He's the Canadian groundhog who comes out every February 2nd to predict whether Canadians will have an early spring. In Wiarton, every time a Willie dies the next groundhog gets the same name.

By the time we pulled into Sauble, my nerves were shot. It was crowded, but what I didn't expect was ferocious winds, enormous waves and a deserted beach. Clearly somebody failed to do their due diligence. Lake Huron, with its rip currents and surfable waves, is nothing like the protected lakes of cottage country.

"This is the worst vacation we have ever been on."

Charlie wasn't wrong, and his declaration was made without malice. The next morning after a bad sleep in a cold, dark cabin with no functioning Wi-Fi as promised, I fled at sunrise to get a photo of the iconic welcome sign. Then I sent my husband Rick for coffee and made an impulsive decision.

"Hello—I know this sounds weird, but we're looking for a last-minute reservation. For today."

It took an hour to clean the cottage, four hours to drive straight to our next destination, and 13 days to get my $300 damage deposit back. We never made it to the Grotto.

"So, it turns out we are not Sauble Beach people," I confessed on Facebook without naming names. "We abandoned our beach-town vacation and decamped to a family-run lodge in Muskoka where I don't have to cook because all the meals are included and where the water is calm and perfect for young swimmers. Also, the Wi-Fi works and so does my cell (serious problems with both in Sauble). Waiting for things to warm up to 22C today."

Nobody gave me a hard time or asked how much money we lost walking away from six nights of a seven-night booking. My friend Ken even went as far as to call my move impressive. "You must be a good poker player," he commented. "You know when to fold 'em. Cut your losses and get the hell out of the hand."

We got lucky with the next hand. The Muskoka lodge was running at partial capacity because of COVID but had a last-minute cancellation for three nights. We rearranged ourselves in the new, smaller space, with a bunkbed in the bedroom and a queen bed in the living room.

I will name names here because parents should know about Shamrock Lodge. The food reminds me (in a good way) of my mom's meals circa 1970, the vibe is mellow, the water is shallow and clear, there's a tiny beach, sandy lake bottom and a heated indoor pool. We took one languid pontoon boat trip around tony Lake Rosseau and gawked at the "cottages" whose boathouses were bigger than the cottage I grew up with.

But there were two catches—one for each child.

Hazel developed a sore throat, which is a big deal in COVID times, and was either lethargic or apathetic. She refused to go swimming, kayaking, canoeing or pedal boating, but happily read and listened to music. I remember being 12.

Charlie was happy at the Shamrock but announced he would only eat in the room.

That's his autism talking. He has been rigid about food since he was born and the doctors thought I wasn't breastfeeding him enough. When we put him in daycare as a toddler, he went on a six-week hunger strike and wouldn't eat anything the staff gave him. He was diagnosed before he was two and is as borderline a case of ASD as there could be. He "passes for normal" and loved the chaos and cacophony of public school, but quietly fell so far behind we moved him to a niche private school for kids with learning and social challenges.

I force travel on my kids. Until this year, we flew to my husband's ranch in Alberta every summer and then road-tripped around Montana, Wyoming, Alberta and Saskatchewan. We pulled the kids out of school one December so I could celebrate my 50th birthday in Cuba. We splurged on Mother's Day 2017 at the Fogo Island Inn and impulsively bought a house on the Newfoundland island just from looking at it from outside. Now we have to fly to our "cottage."

I took Hazel to Clearwater, Florida, with me once for a story about the real dolphin from the *Dolphin Tale* films and we worked such long days she told me she never wanted to travel with me again. Just as the pandemic was shutting down the U.S./Canada border, Charlie was going to join me for work road trip across Arizona, and Hazel was going to come on an island-hopping Hawaii expedition cruise assignment. Any hope that they were finally becoming travellers died when those trips were cancelled.

In Muskoka, the fact that we were all happy in a strange hotel room felt like a victory. Besides, I actually love getting room service and eating in my PJs.

Charlie jumped off the dock at the Shamrock and frolicked in the shallow water. He loved having the indoor pool to himself and racing me across it. But I pushed him too far. Rick got it in his head that we should go tubing and I bribed Charlie to come.

"I'll take you to the store and let you buy any Lego Ninjago that you want."

When we climbed into a three-seat tube, I warned the drivers that Charlie was scared. They showed us the hand signal for "slow down" but took off fast and Charlie started screaming. He wept and wailed in terror for the entire ride, as I tried desperately to signal and held him tightly, covering his head so he didn't have to see the lake speeding and spinning by. I thought for sure he would barf, but he held it in.

We survived and then jumped off the dock a bunch of times to erase the experience from Charlie's mind. He has never mentioned the tubing terror again. And, for the record, Hazel had her first COVID test as soon as we got home, and it was negative.

Sauble was the first getaway I booked during the pandemic summer of 2020, but it wasn't the only trip we took.

There is a place in Prince Edward County that we successfully travelled to twice this summer. It's called Little Ben, an impossibly stylish, one-bedroom cottage on Lake Ontario at the end of the long yard of the house that belongs to our friends Amy and John.

Now this could have been a Sauble Beach situation, because Lake Ontario, like Lake Huron, can be rough and treacherous. We knew to avoid popular Sandbanks Provincial Park in the time of COVID and discovered lesser-known North Beach Provincial Park instead.

This park has two beaches for the price of one. When you drive in, you'll see 1,200 metres of sandy beach facing Lake Ontario and warnings about undertows and dangerous water. Keep driving around the corner into a protected bay where there's another 800 metres of beach that feels like a quiet cottage lake. There's a good amount of clear, shallow water with a sandy bottom before a steep and sudden drop off.

Even Hazel put on a bathing suit here. Rick and Charlie played games in the shallows and I treaded water endlessly in the deep water watching the happy moments from afar. There were small crowds and ample room for social-distanced swimming.

There are other things to love about the County. Ex-Toronto chef Jamie Kennedy's famous hand-cut, twice-fried French fries, sprinkled with sea salt and fresh thyme and now served from his Hillier farm. The particularly delicious roast chickens from Foodland in Wellington. The campfire cream ice cream from Slickers in Bloomfield that is the best version of the burnt marshmallow flavour in Canada.

Fries and ice cream are really all it takes to make my kids into happy travellers, at least for a precious few minutes.

"I'm starting to like this place," Charlie mused at the cottage in late July. He figures so prominently in this summer's travel memories because Lucy stayed home to work and Hazel mostly stayed in her room.

A picture of Charlie falling out a hammock at Little Ben is my favourite image of the summer.

Charlie and I liked swimming from our cottage to "the point," then the "clean beach," then the "secret beach" and back. We took advantage of the fact our family has a nice piece of land at Bain Lake—known locally in the Franco-Ontarian area as Clear Lake because in French "bain" means bath.

I spent my childhood here, loving it when I was little and loathing it as a teenager. Like I said, when I was a single mom with no money for fancy vacations, this is where I brought Lucy and her best friend Rebecca. What I remember most is how the mosquitos that ignored me tortured her and gave her enormous, hive-like welts.

I'm finally old enough to appreciate this place. It's remote (between North Bay and Sudbury) and not part of any big-name cottage region like Muskoka, Haliburton or the Kawarthas. I can see the northern end of the lake from our dock at the south end. The lake used to be busy with anglers, sailors, water skiers and swimmers, but now it's almost dead. We have relatives in the cottages on either side of us, but mindful of COVID we only waved and exchanged a sugar pie for fresh-picked strawberries.

The kids and I sat on the deck feeding peanuts to chipmunks. I told them how I used to catch garter snakes and try to make them my friends, and about polliwogs (big tadpoles just before they transform into frogs). We took time to appreciate a toad, butterflies, dragonflies and one broken robin's egg.

"Do fish bite?" Charlie wondered, and I realized all the things I have failed to teach my urban kids, like how to get in and out a hammock.

The kids were somewhat happy here.

"I don't want to leave the perimeters of the cottage," was Charlie's mantra.

"My mental health needs to be around other kids my age," was Hazel's plea, until I promised to have her home for her friend's socially distant, outdoor birthday gathering.

Sitting alone on the dock, I remembered bringing a small urn of my dad's ashes here and releasing them into the lake after he died in 2001. I felt a sickening stab of guilt. My mom died a year ago and I now have a mini urn of her ashes. I was so busy trying to be a good mom this summer, I failed to be the good daughter who remembers to scatter her mom's ashes.

I didn't keep track of how many barf bags we blew through this summer, but according to my Facebook posts, my family looked healthy and happy as we traipsed about the province. Through all of it, we steered clear of COVID. I wonder how the kids will remember this summer.

"What's your favourite place?" Charlie asked as Labour Day approached.

He knows the answer. We just sold Rick's family ranch, so there won't be any more Alberta bison, coyotes and rattlesnakes in our future. My favourite place is Fogo Island, that island off an island that makes me break my rule about not visiting the same place twice. It's quiet there and never crowded, even when it's full of tourists from around the world. There's one beach, a mysterious herd of caribou, puffins, partridgeberry ice cream and fish and chips. There were also tough travel restrictions this year to keep non-Newfoundlanders away.

"I wish we could go to Fogo," Charlie said at the end of our pandemic summer. He knew this will please me.

"We will, buddy—someday we really will."

* * *

Jennifer Bain is an award-winning, Toronto-based journalist and mother of three who travels the world in search of quirk. She has proudly been to all 10 Canadian provinces and all three territories. Jennifer spent 18 years as food and travel editor at Canada's largest newspaper, the Toronto Star, before going freelance so she could write for a variety of online outlets, magazines and newspapers. She's the author of 111 Places in Calgary That You Must Not Miss, Buffalo Girls Cooks Bison *and the* Toronto Star Cookbook: More Than 150 Diverse & Delicious Recipes Celebrating Ontario. *Jennifer has a journalism degree from Carleton University in Ottawa and an MFA in Creative Nonfiction from the University of King's College in Halifax. Find her portfolio at https://jenniferbain.co and her thoughts on Instagram, Facebook and Twitter as @thesaucylady.*

MOTHERHOOD, LIFE AND KENYA

Carolyn Ray

I'm standing with my daughter in a hot, dusty, schoolyard in Kenya as a wave of children in brightly coloured clothing surges toward us.

Their excitement is palpable, as they shout "Jambo!" (Swahili for hello.) Before I can react, they grasp my hand in theirs and pull me toward a group of brick buildings. I'm surrounded by the happy, smiling faces of children singing joyously. At first, I am uncertain and uncomfortable with their friendliness. Yet here, in a small village in the Masai Mara, just outside of Nairobi in the Great Rift Valley, this warm greeting is commonplace, an authentic expression of welcome.

It's August 2018, and I'm on a service trip with my daughter and other families from across North America. For years, I've had a deep desire to visit Africa, one I often expressed to friends and family. In March, my wish came true when friends in New York invited me to join them on this trip. The timing felt perfect; Alyxandra, my 18-year-old daughter, would start university in the fall, and I hoped that this experience would empower her to make good choices about her education and her future.

Alyx and I have travelled extensively together since she was a small child. I took her on her first international trip, to England, France, and the Netherlands, at age four. She's travelled solo since she was 16 and spent weeks with me travelling throughout Spain. But this trip was different. It wasn't just about the destination; it was about the relationship between mother and daughter.

While I didn't realize it at the time, this experience created an unbreakable bond between us, magnified by a profound, unique and moving experience that would shape our lives in ways I never expected. I thought this trip would give her the courage I never had growing up and the confidence to make her own decisions. I thought the experience would empower her and reinforce how fortunate she was, and it did.

But it did much more than that.

Each day of our 10-day stay in Kenya, we travelled to different communities with our group. We toured elementary schools, a hospital, a farm, several homes, women's colleges, and a Women's Empowerment Centre.

We hauled water jugs, mixed concrete, picked vegetables and learned the art of beading with the Kenyan mamas. We bounced along rocky roads as children of all ages ran excitedly towards our open-air bus, waving frantically, smiling and yelling 'Jambo!'

I learned the importance of introductions—the warm greeting, the clasping of palms, an open smile with direct eye contact. It's a simple and powerful acknowledgement that we are all human beings, that we are all connected. I see you. You see me.

Kenya is a hierarchical culture; men have several wives, and families live together in flat mud huts in small compounds. Cooking and sleeping happens inside the huts, and the wives work together to provide for all the children. Wherever we went, we saw the mamas working together, hauling water, cleaning, laughing and smiling.

As the only single mother on the trip, I stood out a bit from the families we travelled with. This became obvious when we introduced ourselves at the different schools we visited. At one school, standing arm-in-arm with my daughter, I introduced myself as "Mama Carolyn" and said that I owned my own business, which generated a lot of discussion. Alyx said her name but they couldn't pronounce it properly, so she became Alice, which made us both giggle. After oohing and ahhing, the children yelled "Jambo Carolyn! Jambo Alice!" so enthusiastically that it made us laugh. For the rest of the trip, Alyx is now Alice.

In Kenya, education is a privilege. The older girls live away from home and adhere to an incredibly rigorous schedule that starts before 5 a.m. and lasts until 10 p.m. They study science, math, and English. I was amazed to learn that they are taught about values such as 'enjoy every moment' and 'be grateful'. Behind one of the schools, we visited a small mud hut, where the girls go when they are homesick. They are so young, and so far from their families. I was inspired by their courage.

At one school, I mentioned that I taught at a university a few years ago. The principal's eyes light up as he told a group of children that I was a teacher. Suddenly, I was surrounded by young smiling faces who grasped my palms, hugged me, and said thank you. Again, I am overwhelmed.

Teachers are revered in Kenya. They are the path to knowledge and a better life. In Kenya, most children only go to school until they are in grade six. At every school, we told the children how proud we are of them for pursuing an education. "Stay in school," we say. "Keep learning!"

At the colleges, the older girls were intensely curious about our lives in Canada. Do we go to school? Do we have a library? Do we have a pet? What music do we listen to? What do we eat? What kind of house do we live in? Alyx found she has more in common with them than she thought. They knew who Justin Bieber is. They used computers. As we toured a farm, the girls told her the names of each plant and vegetable, in multiple languages. My daughter was awe-struck.

We were astonished by the ambition of the college girls. When I asked one of the young women at the college why she wanted to be a nurse, she told me of a young disabled person in her village, and how she wanted to help them have a better life. These young girls aspired to be nurses, teachers, agriculturalists, engineers.

Alyx was deeply affected by their courage, and by the strength of their family and community bonds.

These girls were curious about the world, but it was more important to them to bring their knowledge back to serve their families and communities. This is a generosity of spirit at its best; when we do things not for ourselves, but for others.

During our journey, Alyx and I cried, laughed and hugged each other constantly. The simplest things affected us. I smiled so much that my face hurt. I often found myself in tears without really knowing why.

Each day we shared our thoughts. What impacted us? What moment broke through that veneer of Western expectation? I found it hard to articulate complex emotions in words and I fumble. I'm overwhelmed, uninspiring and incoherent.

The young people in our group didn't hesitate to express their feelings. One young woman captured my sentiments perfectly, bringing tears to my eyes when she said: "Living at home, we have clean water, a closet full of clothes, electricity and abundant food. Before I came here, I looked at Africa and pitied them. But that's wrong. We can learn so much from them. They only know gratitude, joy, humility and happiness."

It was one of the most profound things I heard on our trip, from a 14-year-old.

There are so many lessons and shifts that happen when you travel, and their impact can take time to process and last long after the journey has ended.

On our last night in Kenya, Alyx and I wondered how we could bring our lessons from Kenya back home with us. We were ready to be the change; we just didn't know what to change. As we flew back to Nairobi over the lush, green hills, watching giraffes run below us, I wondered how I could ever share the effect of this experience with friends and family.

A few weeks later, back in Toronto, I had an opportunity to do this in a way I never imagined.

My house, which had been on the market for months, suddenly sold. This was a sign—a chance to reinvent my life.

As I looked around my home, I realized that I'd been trained to acquire material possessions. That I had spent hours and days searching for that one perfect thing to put in my house. With Alyx leaving for university, I was going to be alone, surrounded by furniture and knick-knacks, not people. I was overcome with guilt, realizing that I had wasted precious time I could have spent with my daughter, or writing, or practicing self-care. Instead I had been accumulating things.

In that moment, I decided I want to be free. I got rid of everything I owned. The things I'd stored for over 20 years. My grandparents' furniture. Antiques. Clothing I no longer wore; items I didn't need.

I donated my clothing, shoes, coats, and boots to charities. I drove to a part of Toronto I'd never been to and donated what felt like frivolous formal wear to a local boutique, imagining a young teenager at her first prom in one of my dresses. It made me smile.

By mid-October, my house was empty. I rented a small storage unit for some beloved antique furniture, family heirlooms and musical instruments, including a 120-year-old piano made by my great-grandfather. I moved into a furnished rental apartment and gave back my leased car. I was possession-free, and it felt like the world opened up to me. I embraced the feeling of being able to put everything I owned in a backpack to travel the world.

Through this experience, my definition of home has been redefined. I once thought of home as the place where you have all your stuff. Now I know that home is where my family is.

After our trip, Alyx chose her courses at university, which included women's studies and global development. Now in her third year, she is considering becoming a lawyer because she has realized that she can help protect women who may not have a voice. "There are many people who need people and organizations to help them fight for their human rights," she said. I'm beside myself with pride.

Our journey to Africa opened our minds and freed our spirits. I never imagined the impact this experience would have on me and my daughter. I've tried to replicate the simplicity I witnessed in Africa in my own life. I feel free, empowered and grateful. I know that this is a gift.

The community I met in Kenya and the one I've fostered at home through the acquisition of JourneyWoman helped change my life and connected me with others who share my passion for travel. The emotional connections we made in Kenya—the touch of a hand, a genuine, welcoming smile, looking into a young person's eyes— these are my greatest memories of our time in Africa. Remembering these moments and respecting different ways of life are what I will always try to bring with me, no matter where I travel to.

I may not get it all right, but I intend to keep trying and to bring the lessons from the people of the Masai Mara into my life.

Jambo!

* * *

Carolyn Ray has spent her career advocating for women. She's an entrepreneur, a single mother, a leadership coach to women, and a SheEO Activator, mentoring women-owned businesses. In 2019, she was invited to continue the legacy of the beloved women's travel magazine, JourneyWoman, by Erica Ehm, daughter of the late Evelyn Hannon, the original JourneyWoman, who inspired a generation of women to travel solo. After 10 years at brand strategy firm Interbrand, most recently as the Canadian CEO, Carolyn started her own firm in 2017. She serves on the Board of Directors for the non-profit group Myseum of Toronto and the Society of American Travel Writers (SATW) and is a member of the Travel Media Association of Canada (TMAC). She was ranked as one of Canada's top 100 female entrepreneurs on the 2013 PROFIT/ Chatelaine W100 list.

HIKING TO MEET THE SUN

Maia Selkirk

At two a.m., the cool night air was a welcome change from the heat of the past week. I tried to get dressed quietly so as not to wake up my parents, but they stirred as I pulled on my boots. They waved goodbye and my mum muttered something about remembering to take lots of pictures. I slipped out the door and closed it quietly behind me.

We were in Dalhousie, in the Central Province of Sri Lanka, and I was going to climb Sri Pada. Also known as Adam's Peak, the 2,243-metre mountain resembles a large footprint when seen from above. Depending on which tradition you subscribe to, it's the footprint of Buddha, Lord Shiva, or Adam.

I was hiking it to see the sunrise. Thousands of pilgrims climb it each day. It's a holy place. At the top, there's a shrine to Saman—the patron deity of the mountain.

The mountain is always moving, a thin snake of climbers coming up and down, weaving across the densely forested slope. People make the climb at all hours of the night and day and the mountain is home to many small snack shops and tea houses for climbers to rest at. When you look at the mountain, the side is dotted with a line of lights. They stop about halfway up. Past that, it's too difficult to trek supplies up.

I was thirteen and climbing with some family friends that were joining us on our trip through Sri Lanka. Faced with the prospect of five thousand steps at two in the morning, my parents had declined and told me to have fun by myself. Sounds awful, they told me. Good luck.

To me, the cold air was charged with the excitement of waking up too early on Christmas morning. I was filled with energy, and

I bounced lightly as our group made its way to the trailhead. It felt like a procession. We followed wizened old women in saris and bare feet, tall young backpackers with cameras, and small children clutching their parents' hands. At the base of the mountain a monk tied a white string around my wrist and smiled at me. Despite the crowds, it was quiet. It was a strange, anticipatory hush, like we were all waiting for someone. I didn't want to breathe too loudly.

We began to climb, and my bounciness wore off. The trail we took was the most popular one, but the friends I was hiking with climbed at a fast pace and we soon left the busy parts behind us. We sped up the stairs that made up the trail and I focused carefully on where I placed my feet. The closely packed snack shops started to spread out, and in the darkness, I started to worry.

The year before, I'd injured my ankle badly. I'd damaged the tendon and joint to the point that my physiotherapist had whistled when he'd first seen me and asked how I'd managed to walk around on it for so long. I'd been going to weekly physiotherapy for six months, right up until we left Australia, where we were living at the time. As we climbed, my ankle began to shake, and twinges started to shoot up my calf muscles. My foot and ankle were securely strapped into a heavy-duty brace, but the climb would take us about three hours. I started to lag behind the group.

I grew up travelling with my parents. We left our home in Vancouver, Canada, when I was seven to sail around the world. Sailing had always been my parents' dream, but I loved the opportunities for travel that it afforded me, even if I could do without the constant sand and salt. In Sri Lanka, we'd decided to travel inland, and it was my first experience of a more independent way to travel. I wandered through small shops and markets with the other young teenagers that we were travelling with, and I learned to see places through my own eyes, rather than my parents'. Though I didn't admit it at the time, it's one of the reasons I was so insistent on doing the hike alone. I wanted to know what it was like to do things by myself.

The air started to thin and I wished for my inhaler. In retrospect, I was perhaps not in the best shape to do the hike—my wonky ankle and my asthma—but I had always been stubborn, and there were little old ladies making the climb. Of course I could do it. The group noticed I was dropping behind. One of the women turned to me. I felt awful. We'd agreed that we would hike for the sunrise, knowing that we needed to move at a fairly quick pace in order to make it to the summit on time.

"What do you want to do?" she asked me.

Although the tea houses were less frequent now, there were still a few scattered up the trail. Ignoring the pain in my ankle, I hurried after the group until we reached the next set of lights.

To call it a tea house was generous. It was a small hut of corrugated metal, and several plastic chairs were sat in front. I took a seat, and the group left. It was cold. Later, I checked the temperature and learned it had been about ten degrees Celsius, which would have been fine had I not been wearing shorts and a light jumper, more prepared for a brisk hike than a night spent sitting outside.

The door to the tea house creaked open, and an elderly man emerged. He was patient with me as I stumbled through the basic Sinhalese in my guidebook. He nodded at me encouragingly and disappeared back into his house. A few minutes later, he emerged with a cup of sweet black tea. It was very strong, and I held it in my hands and pulled my knees up under my jumper like a child, trying to conserve heat. He looked concerned and went back into his house. I sipped my tea and rocked from side to side in my plastic chair, starting to stiffen from the climb and the cold. My ankle ached.

At some point he came back, followed by his wife, who reached out to feel my cheek and made a sound that is universally familiar—the tut that mothers give when children are doing something stupid.

"Come in," she said. "It's far too cold outside."

From an outside perspective, following a couple into their house deep in the woods at 3 a.m. is not the best move. But I had an unusual upbringing. My parents taught me things like trusting my gut, and reading body language, and how to know if someone's lying about what they want from you. I grew up trusting the kindness of strangers. These people had good hands, and open eyes.

The house was very small. It was one room, and about a quarter of the room was taken up by a broad bed, piled with blankets, and a small lump in the corner that looked to be another person. There was a battery-powered lamp that sat on a shelf and I could see a kettle and a stack of foam cups next to a bag of loose tea.

"My sister," the woman explained, pointing at the person in the corner, and patted the bed.

She pulled back a swathe of blankets and pointed at my shoes. I kicked them off and climbed in, and she climbed in after me, giving me a last pat on the cheek and wishing me good night. Her husband climbed in after her, and the wooden platform that made up the bed creaked a little. In the morning, she told me, my friends would come, and I would be warm enough to hike down the mountain. It was time to sleep.

The next morning, I was woken with a hot cup of tea from my hosts. I hadn't had a chance to see the beauty of the mountain in the darkness of the previous night, but as I stepped outside, I was overcome with green. Everything was lush and lovely. One of the mythologies of the mountain tells that it was the first place that Adam set foot when he was cast out from the Garden of Eden. As I looked around, it seemed a good place to end up. The mountain was an Eden all of its own. I liked the idea of it. It seemed a good place to find shelter, as I had learned, and I imagined Adam finding comfort on the mountain just as I had.

There was a steady stream of pilgrims coming up and down the trail, and behind me, the man and woman were busy setting up their tea house for the day—they set out packets of peanut brittle and started to boil water. I helped put out more chairs for the influx of tired tourists. The sun had come up and I knew my friends would be leaving soon, but I wasn't worried. My ankle felt better, and I was warmer now.

Once everything was ready for the day, I sat with the couple. The language barrier was hard to cross, but we managed. I explained that I was Canadian, that I was travelling with my parents. They brought out a few photos, worn around the edges. It was their daughter, they told me. She had moved to Canada. They wondered if I knew her. They said that when they next wrote her, they would tell her that they had helped someone from her adopted country. I nodded and I tried to explain how much their help had meant to me.

Beyond the fact that they had kept me warm and sheltered, they had kept me trusting. I had wanted a taste of independence, and that could have gone very badly, were it not for the kindness of strangers. As I had sat at the tea house alone, I had missed my parents terribly, but the no nonsense warmth of my hosts had made it easy to fall asleep.

I didn't know how to convey this, so instead I smiled, and I helped the woman fold up the extra blankets while her husband got breakfast for her sister, who was bedbound.

Soon after, I spotted my dad climbing the trail. He was moving quickly, and he nearly passed the house before I shouted after him, and he stopped, breaking into a smile. He hugged me tightly. He'd brought warm clothes up the mountain with him. Our friends had managed to get a phone signal at the top of the mountain, he explained, and told him what had happened. I introduced him to the couple.

They seemed slightly suspicious of this man that would let his young daughter hike a mountain in the middle of the night, but they shook his hand as he thanked them seriously. The woman saw the camera that my dad had hooked around his shoulder. My mum had told him to take it, he said. If he was going to have to hike the damn mountain, he might as well get some good pictures.

"Will you take a photo of us?" she asked quietly.

The photo that he took shows me sitting between them—we're all smiling up at the camera, and the clothes of my hosts were a riot of colour in the early morning light. She was wearing a bright blue skirt and he was wearing a yellow sweater. Behind us, the greenery outshines us.

I'd left the little money I had in my bag under one of their pillows, back in their house, and I felt guilty that I didn't have more to give them. I thanked them for taking care of me, and the woman patted my cheek as she hugged me goodbye.

Have a safe trip, she told me. Be careful of your ankle. Be careful where you step.

The way back down the mountain was easy, with the sun at my back and a sturdy walking stick that my father had found for me along the trail.

"How was your adventure?" my dad asked me as we paused so he could take some pictures. "All by yourself?"

"It was good," I told him. "I think you and mum taught me how to travel well."

My dad smiled at me. "No more family trips?"

"I don't think I'm ready to set off alone yet," I said, and I reached out to hold his hand.

* * *

Maia Selkirk is a nineteen-year-old Canadian-American who grew up sailing around the world with her parents. After sailing for eight years, through 35 different countries, Maia and her family settled back down in their home city of Vancouver, Canada. After a year of land life, she took off at seventeen to move to the Kingdom of Eswatini to finish high school at the United World College of Southern Africa and obtain her International Baccalaureate diploma. Maia loves to write, has blogged extensively about her travels, and had her work published in several magazines.

ACKNOWLEDGEMENTS

It may not take a village to raise a book but producing this one has certainly benefitted from many helping hands and cheerleading individuals along the way.

I must begin with thanks to early supporters Christopher Flett and Heather White, who nurtured my creative writing visions and helped me down the path that led to this particular destination. Thank you also to Kathy Buckworth and Annemarie Tempelman-Kluit for advice about the world of publishing.

Gratitude to Ann-Marie Metten of Historic Joy Kogawa House in Vancouver, who over bowls of green curry and pad thai, embraced my idea for this anthology with enthusiasm and offered continued support throughout the process. Through Ann-Marie, I met my publisher and editor Michael Mirolla. Sincere thanks to Michael and his team at Guernica Editions based in Hamilton, Ontario, for their assistance and support.

I benefitted from participating in Pandemic University writing workshops, particularly those sessions on narrative structure, getting personal, and mastering conflict, which were delivered so well in the early days of COVID-era Zoom seminars, by Jana Pruden, Hadiya Roderique and Ayelet Tsabari.

I'm grateful to my friend Alec Scott for his support and for reviewing first drafts with a kindness that was morale-boosting. Heartfelt gratitude to Don George for his analysis and valued literary advice, and to Rainer Jenss of the Family Travel Association for sharing his thoughts in the foreword. Special thanks to Lola Akinmade Åkerström and Andrew McCarthy.

Hugs of gratitude to the lovely and talented Lavinia Spalding, a mentor of many years whose words and storytelling abilities never fail to inspire. Her generous support was priceless.

I am so grateful to the fabulous collection of writers who agreed to share and entrust to me their wonderful stories in this anthology. Thank you to Lucas Aykroyd, Jennifer Bain, Sabine Bergmann, Yvonne Blomer, Heather Greenwood Davis, Lynn Easton, Robin Esrock, Helen Gowans, Carolyn B. Heller, Bruce Kirkby, Grant Lawrence, Jessica Wynne Lockhart, Jenn Smith Nelson, Carolyn Ray, Alec Scott, Diane Selkirk, Maia Selkirk, Lavinia Spalding, and Olivia Stren.

Finally, love and gratitude to my parents, Kathi and Emilio Campana for instilling in me a passion for travel and gracing me with a fortunate and memorable childhood. All of my love to my husband Stephane Laroye and my kids Sebastien and Nicolas for believing in me and allowing me to do the necessary work in producing this book. And for all our past and future adventures together.

"You can't buy happiness, but you can buy ice cream and that is pretty much the same thing."